SAGE was founded in 1965 by Sara Miller McCune to support the dissemination of usable knowledge by publishing innovative and high-quality research and teaching content. Today, we publish over 900 journals, including those of more than 400 learned societies, more than 800 new books per year, and a growing range of library products including archives, data, case studies, reports, and video. SAGE remains majority-owned by our founder, and after Sara's lifetime will become owned by a charitable trust that secures our continued independence.

Los Angeles | London | New Delhi | Singapore | Washington DC | Melbourne

Her-Self

Her-Self
Gender and Early Writings of
Malayali Women, 1898–1938

Translated from the Malayalam
and edited by
J. Devika

Los Angeles | London | New Delhi
Singapore | Washington DC | Melbourne

Copyright © J. Devika, 2021

All rights reserved. No part of this book may be reproduced or utilized in any form or by any means, electronic or mechanical, including photocopying, recording, or by any information storage or retrieval system, without permission in writing from the publisher.

First published by STREE, an imprint of Bhatkal and Sen, 16 Southern Avenue, Kolkata 700026 in 2005.

This edition published in 2021 by

SAGE Publications India Pvt Ltd
B1/I-1 Mohan Cooperative Industrial Area
Mathura Road, New Delhi 110 044, India
www.sagepub.in

STREE
16 Southern Avenue
Kolkata 700 026
www.stree-samyabooks.com

SAGE Publications Inc
2455 Teller Road
Thousand Oaks, California 91320, USA

SAGE Publications Ltd
1 Oliver's Yard, 55 City Road
London EC1Y 1SP, United Kingdom

SAGE Publications Asia-Pacific Pte Ltd
18 Cross Street #10-10/11/12
China Square Central
Singapore 048423

Published by Vivek Mehra for SAGE Publications India Pvt Ltd. Typeset in 11/13pt Baskerville by Fidus Design Pvt Ltd, Chandigarh.

Library of Congress Control Number: 2021939473

ISBN: 978-93-81345-67-2 (PB)

SAGE Stree Team: Aritra Paul, Amrita Dutta and Neena Ganjoo
Cover Design: Swarna Jana

To the loving memory
of my grandmother
Njavarakkal Devaki Amma

Thank you for choosing a SAGE product!
If you have any comment, observation or feedback,
I would like to personally hear from you.

Please write to me at **contactceo@sagepub.in**

Vivek Mehra, Managing Director and CEO, SAGE India.

Bulk Sales

SAGE India offers special discounts
for purchase of books in bulk.
We also make available special imprints
and excerpts from our books on demand.

For orders and enquiries, write to us at

Marketing Department
SAGE Publications India Pvt Ltd
B1/I-1, Mohan Cooperative Industrial Area
Mathura Road, Post Bag 7
New Delhi 110044, India

E-mail us at **marketing@sagepub.in**

Subscribe to our mailing list
Write to **marketing@sagepub.in**

This book is also available as an e-book.

Contents

Foreword: Texts That Dazzle by V. Geetha   xi
Preface to This Edition   xxi
Acknowledgements   xxv
Introduction   xxvii

1. The Demerits of Female Education:
   A Refutation
   N. A. Amma   1

2. Manly Duty
   K. Lakshmy Amma   6

3. An Account of My Life and My Homemaking
   Manntaraveetil Lakshmy Amma   10

4. Are Women Weak?
   K. P. M.   23

5. The Place of Women in Education
   K. Chinnamma   30

6. The Craze for Imitation
   C. P. Kalyani Amma   38

7. 'Modern Women and Their Husbands':
   A Rejoinder
   Mrs. K. Kannan Menon   44

8. Literature and Womankind
   K. M. Kunhulakshmy Kettilamma   50

9. Womanliness
   Sarojini   54

10. Women and Freedom (Part One)
    B. Pachi Amma   63

11. Malayali Marriage Modified
    K. Padmavaty Amma   69

12. The Place of Women in Society
    Vengalil K. Chinnammalu Amma   77

13. An Appeal to the Hindu Women of Kerala
    Vatakkecharuvil P. K. Kalyani   86

14. Nair Women and the Home
    Konniyoor K. Meenakshi Amma   91

15. A Reply
    Tottaikkattu Madhavi Amma   96

16. Our Women
    Mrs. I. C. Chacko   99

17. Women's Independence
    K. Mary Thomas   110

18. Will Not Women Awake?
    Editorial   113

19. On Women's Freedom
    Anna Chandy   117

20. Women and Khadar
    Elamkuttil Narayanikutty Amma   134

21. Women and Literature
    B. Bhageeraty Amma   139

22. Womanliness
    Parvati Nenminimangalam   152

23. Women Should Not Abandon the Kitchen
    Narikkatiri Devaki Antharjanam   155

24. Our Economic Position and Women
    Pennammabhayi, Chambakkulam   158

CONTENTS | ix

25. On Womanly Duty
    Parvaty Ayyappan — 162

26. Womenfolk and Reform: Matters Necessary and Unnecessary
    Ittichiriyamma — 165

27. Our Duty
    Ayesha Mayan — 169

28. Welcome Speech
    M. Haleema Beevi — 171

29. Some Obstacles in the Way of Equality between the Sexes
    Kochattil Kalyanikutty Amma — 177

References and Additional Readings — 183
About the Editor-Translator — 189

Foreword

Texts That Dazzle

This is a world of ideas that thinking women in Kerala made available to their contemporaries in the late 1890s and during the first three decades of the twentieth century. Voiced and written in the context of debates about women's education, duties, vocation and civic roles these were informed initially by reformist ideas and subsequently by nationalist and communist assumptions about the greater common good. These views comprise arguments that continue to haunt feminist thinking and gender studies to this day.

The themes rehearsed in this book of distinctive male and female roles, the enabling power and authority of feminist duties and virtues, the transcendent claims of individual intelligence over bodily destiny, the vexed question of gendered identity, the conflicting claims of home and the world have been the subject of endless feminist debates across the world. And it is through adding their own to these contentious matters and providing a specific historical gloss on them that these texts dazzle.

The manner and style in which these speeches and essays map their arguments, counter objections, and advance their theses are well captured in Devika's competent translation—her introductory note embeds them in the history that produced them. Devika resists overstatement and elaborate theorizing, and her lucid elucidation of the discursive as well as the historical contexts of particular texts is commendable. Her argument inflects well-known historical themes in interesting ways: we see, for instance, how the peculiar condition of princely rule, as well as the specific details of

Nair matriliny, re-figured late colonial concerns about the status of women, their education, aspirations for freedom, work and so on. This was especially evident in the manner in which Nair women re-worked notions of the domestic and the public: working within Nair reformism, and yet drawing on their experiences—and memories of an active domestic life (see, for example, the essays by Vengalil K. Chinnammalu Amma and C. P. Kalyani Amma). One, of course, always wishes for more, for instance, on how Gandhi and Gandhian ideas were appropriated and transformed by nationalist women in Ketala; on the historical shift, however gradual, which moved discussions about education and reform of customs to being debates on women's civic and national roles.

What I propose to do here is to essay a contrary move: lift these texts out of their constitutive historical moment and consider them in the context of larger and more global arguments about women's rights to equality and justice and the social and political arrangements that these rights claims demanded and mandated. There is a rich history of ideas here that waits to be written, and I hope to gesture somewhat in that direction.

The texts in this collection may be grouped thus: texts which assert women's right to learning and are dismissive of those arguments that insist women are not suited for it; texts which argue for an expansive public role for women and re-state the relationship between the domestic and the public spheres; texts which seek to re-write the social as well as the sexual contracts of their times and, finally those which address issues of a greater common good, transcending caste and faith.

The texts that engage with learning and education resonate with other texts of the period, and even earlier, for example, Pandita Ramabai's injunctions on the importance of female learning. More important, the reasons advanced by the writers in this volume for women's education are similar to those voiced by eighteenth-and nineteenth centuries'

Anglo-European feminists, who were also wrestling with a recalcitrant male intelligentsia, determined to argue women out of scholarly pursuits. One of the common ruses resorted to by Victorian gentlemen who were aghast at women wanting to read was to claim that such an exercise of the mind's energy would de-feminize women, in fact, shrink their wombs, for women were biologically unstable and could not be trusted to receive rational thought with the discretion it deserved. We find variations of this argument in early modern Kerala as well. The responses to such reasoning were dismissive; charges of male hypocrisy were routinely advanced to disprove men's lofty arguments in a manner reminiscent of Tarabai Shinde who unpacked male prejudices in her *Stri Purush Tulana* (A Comparison between Women and Men). They were also unexpected: through an astonishing invocation of women's experience of menstruation, N. A. Amma (writing in 1897) observed that such processes as these which perhaps caused men to believe women were unstable were actual cleansing processes and resulted ultimately in women being healthy and well. So men need not fear that women's bodies would militate their acquisition of knowledge.

Other women worked with the well-known trope that educating women would only make better wives and mothers but the question needs to be asked, if this was not an enabling rhetorical detail in these debates, rather than an idea. For this and the related idea that the world outside where women sought their place was, in reality, an extension of the family were as much rhetorical counterpoints as they were ideological statements.

Women thinkers sought to link literary earning and skills with female progress—not surprising in a context where literary experimentation went hand in hand with a liberal point of view (not merely in Kerala but in nearby Tamil Nadu as well, where the novel became the carrier of critical social ideas). Yet these reflections were accented differently by women, as is evident from K. M. Kunhulakshmy Kettilamma's linking of social freedom with literary talent: 'How can any effort that relies upon indirect experience that has not the strength derived from delving into the labyrinthine complexities, the twists and turns of the ways of the world, prove fecund? Mental faculties develop only when there is freedom of action. Is it not said that "action influences the intelligence, but the intelligence does not influence action"?' This is wonderfully provocative, for certain strands of English feminist literary theory have attempted to claim for literary expressions of women's uniquely limited experiences a validity all their own.

Others looked to link literature and female experience differently. B. Bhageeraty Amma, for example, considered the status of women and Malayalam literature to be analogous to each other and argued that in the course of history both had become subject to degradation and had to be redeemed. Her exhortations to linguistic purity were intrinsically gendered: she argued, just like Tamil women (and some men) did during the anti-Hindi campaigns of the late 1930s, that miscegenation was a crime that was bound to destroy both language and blood. Interestingly, though her arguments remain only logically and ethically linked, she did not apostrophize Malayalam as a virginal woman, as Tamil enthusiasts of the late 1940s and afterwards would of Tamil. Yet her writings force us to think through issues of gender, genre and the nation carefully.

Sometimes these affirmations of the value of learning served to launch a larger demand: an enhanced public role for women. This was expressed in several ways. In a curious re-aligning of the relationship between the home and the world, Vengalil K. Chinnamallu Amma noted that women possessed a greater sense of the sanctity of life—she noted that Gandhari felt the pangs of death and destruction in Kurukshetra more than her husband, King Dhritharashtra—and therefore could fulfil certain civic tasks well, public health and hygiene, for one. This was not merely a call to exercise domestic virtues in the public world, but an implicit recognition of a social reality where, as Devika has noted, it was not possible to keep the home and the world apart anymore.

Others insisted on a greater civic role for women of different reasons. Writing in 1935, Parvaty Ayyappan claimed: 'Nature has nurtured in individuals certain instincts for the preservation of the race. Particular sorts of male-female relationships have been shaped through the stirrings of such instincts. The Husband-Wife relationship and the modern domestic life are the cultured versions of these. Women and men have many duties to fulfil that go well beyond them. Women and men must labour alike for the progress of humanity.'

Here we find an invocation of citizenship that is dismissive of the constraints of marriage and motherhood and which seeks to anchor women's public responsibilities in a general edict: that women and men must labour alike, especially now that women can cultivate their minds and avail of birth control. Remarkably similar arguments were voiced by the self-respecters in Tamil Nadu around the same time.

The demand to participate in public life was also advanced in and through critical arguments which challenged male prejudices and attitudes with respect to women's roles and demanded a re-writing of the social contract, as if to say that men must not assume that it is their sole prerogative to be freely active in public. K. Lakshmy Amma wrote: 'Woman is not merely a child producing machine. . . . Is it because no one insists upon Manly Duty that Mankind remains utterly ungrateful to Womankind, who toil all the time for the comfort of their husbands, disregarding their own distress? . . . Is it not proper that Man, who feels the need for freedom, should also feel it necessary to grant it to Woman? Or, is Man's freedom merely a means of bolstering the slavery of Woman?'

Such indignant responses served also to re-structure the terms of the sexual contract that undergirds the social contract, to paraphrase Carol Pateman, and constructs the civic as a compact between men, which required delegating women to the inner world of domestic and sexual servitude. In a brilliant refusal of marriage on the grounds that it cannot serve its purpose in the absence of love between the partners, K. Padmavaty Amma desconstructed as well as abandoned the instrumental nature of the sexual contract: 'If you do not find a bridegroom whom you like and is worthy of you, then it is better to live either in the service of your parents who have cared for you and protected you from all difficulties to earn divine blessings, or educate yourselves as much as your intelligence and situation will permit, to gain appropriate employment. In this way, to hang on to the foolish belief that wifehood alone encapsulates Womanly Duty, to bob about aimlessly in this Ocean of Worldliness full of worry, disease and want, and thus destroy one's life, in this universe that contains many different paths to hither-worldly happiness and other-worldly salvation, is nothing less than a great crime.'

Some went further. B. Pachi Amma argued that marriages where women's choices did not matter automatically rendered even the tacit sexual contract that men assume as unworkable. 'For women file for maintenance because their husbands have not been caring, because their husbands have heartlessly abandoned them. If women are filing for divorce, that is because they were given no say in their marriages, and because the grooms' eligibility was never seriously assessed. Therefore, if marriage has become the bouncing ball of the judiciary, the fault does not lie with women.'

For women like the famous Anna Chandy, participation in public life meant that women could work, enjoy unrestricted access to a labour of their choice. Refusing to accede to the male reformer who insisted on making a woman's marital status the basis for determining her access to employment, she wondered aloud if women who desired to work should therefore be denied the joys of love and a familial existence.

Interestingly she does not argue, as one would expect her to, that work will not de-feminize women. Rather, through a skilful rhetorical move, she neatly de-links love and marriage from work and domesticity. She also re-states the relationship between labour and femininity by invoking an expansive world of work, which awaits women and is necessary for their progress.

Even as they demanded that men unlearn their prejudices, these women thinkers interrogated norms of Womanliness, which after all, had been used to legitimize the idea that domestic care was a woman's chief vocation. In a marvellously deconstructive account of Womanliness, Sarojini pointed out that this was a trait demanded of women by men who wished them to be passive supplicants. But women must know better, she insisted: 'If poets, novelists and their adoring and compliant readership fail to see that Womanliness does not abide in a body that melts like fresh butter in the labour room of a noble mansion, in silk from China, upper cloths from Kottar, or diplomas from universities, at least other women ought to recognize it.' She also went on to observe that Womanliness was not a function of an unfathomable feminine heart, as even every street brat would have it, rather it inhered in a woman's steadfast resolve and firmness of mind.

Not content with criticizing the terms of the social and sexual contracts which limited women's access to the world outside their homes, some, Kochattil Kalyanikutti Amma, in this case, asked for a re-making of the contract on the basis of an equality that does not render all distinctions irrelevant: 'Women who advocate the equality of the sexes do not certainly want one single model to suit everyone. On the contrary, only equality will nurture uniquely individual qualities. We still possess only incomplete knowledge of our natures and dispositions. What do we actually mean by vague terms like "Manliness" and "Womanliness"? Does not research into psychology reveal our ignorance regarding aspects of sex difference? How many individuals are left stunted by our moral precepts, which are the offspring of our half-baked knowledge! In human society with rational orientation, we should behave more considerate towards each other. There, neither class nor caste nor position would matter; the greatness of the mind will form the sole criterion of valuation.' Recalling the eighteenth-century European feminists' trust in the 'tocsin of reason' this good faith in rational intelligence trusted to the discoveries of technology that equalized labour conditions for women and men, and to the marvels of contraception to enable women take their equal and rightful place in the world.

Much of the discussion around equality, freedom and women's rights to a civic existence involved upper caste women either from the Nair or the Kerala Brahmin communities. But there were lone voices that asked for not merely women's rights to a dignified civic existence, but for a transformation of civic life itself. Writing on women's roles in the Vaikom satyagraha, Vatakkecharuvil P. K. Kalyani observed that it was a shame that in this matter of claiming equal rights of access to all castes to the temple streets, upper caste women did not appear to play a role. It would be useful here to recall the Tamil self-respecters; injunctions to upper caste women that they treat their untouchable sisters better. Kalyani's observations may be taken to be an immanent critique of early Malayali feminism, a marking of its limits.

Muslim women desired a different transformation of the civic: in her call to Muslim women to participate in national life, Haleema Beevi pointed out that the Koran enjoined equality and that the Prophet was himself the harbinger of this radical parity between the sexes. Therefore it behove Muslim women to step out of their homes and set their seal on national politics, by becoming a part of it. This neat manner of reconciling secular responsibilities with religious faith serves as a useful counter position to the emerging Hindu Right's rhetoric of the nation and faith, which, among other things, led to the partitioning of the subcontinent. This speech also points to the unfinished task of working through the texts and histories which encapsulate Muslim experiences of the modern, especially modern gender.

These texts are part of our feminist genealogy and need to be read as such—not as testimonies to a greater or lesser political correctness, but as part of a past that is at once local and global.

Chennai   V. Geetha

Preface to This Edition

My memories of painstaking search in musty old libraries and archives were still fresh when I first approached Mandira Sen of Stree Samya around 2004, with a proposal to translate selected essays written by women who could be arguably viewed as the 'first-generation feminists' of Malayali society. As a feminist aspiring to generate critical feminist public discourse in Malayalam, I was awestruck by the brilliance of their rhetoric and penetrating insight into the many layers of the patriarchy of their own times. But even as I was intensely aware, already, of the fact that the feminists of the twenty-first century would have to strive to overthrow much of precisely what they had built, I was left dewy-eyed by the manner in which they caught resonances of feminism from elsewhere in India and the Anglo-American world.

In the more than twenty-five years after I first came across their writings, I have learnt a great deal more about the first generation feminists. More importantly, my understanding of the genealogies of feminism in Malayali society and the time-period in which we have habitually situated the Malayali first generation feminists (the decades of the late nineteenth and early twentieth century) have changed quite significantly. The latter is usually referred to as *Navoddhanam*, or 'Renaissance'—evidently a borrowing from the historical experience of Europe—and refers to the recovery and reinterpretation of classical (largely Hindu) texts. The learnings of the past twenty years, however, convince me that the experience of social change in Malayali society of this period is not exhausted by this characterization, and worse, it authorizes majoritarian interpretations of the period. I prefer now to call the complex and varied social change of this time by the collective name *Vankadayal*—the Great Churning—and the great upsurge of the oppressed communities towards liberation, the *Mahaturavi*—the Great Opening—keeping the two analytically distinct. I also see now that the *Mahaturavi* was not necessarily a thrust toward greater secularization of society but often a search for liberating, enabling, new spirituality that could heal the inner conflicts and divisions of the emergent modern self and society.

Most importantly, I now perceive many genealogies for Malayali feminism which make it local and cosmopolitan. Indeed, this genealogy enables us to address many of the challenges that mainstream feminism in India now faces, for example, that of developing intersectional analyses of patriarchal oppression and reimagining anti-patriarchal struggles intersectionally. The genealogy of anti-patriarchal struggle in Kerala reaches right back to the late eighteenth and early nineteenth centuries, and may be understood in terms of a subaltern concept of resistance: *streevashi* ('the obduracy of women'). This refers to the indomitably persistent acts of defiance, especially by the worst abjected groups of the traditional order of caste of those times, the order of *janmabhedam* or difference-by-birth: Dalit women whose incessant labour was denied humanity and who were treated as productive chattels. Women of the Malayala Brahmin community who were abjected, in a different way, as reproductive chattels. Through the nineteenth-century struggles by the Channar women for dress that signified caste dignity even at the risk of irking their mentors, the missionaries, who preferred them to struggle primarily for modesty. Through the literary retrieval of Malayala Brahmin women who struggled resolutely against their unspeakable dehumanization in the Brahmin homesteads in the writings of Lalithambika. Through the staunch struggles of women workers who were often the initiators of resistance in modern cashew factories and in the fields, one could perhaps trace a genealogy of streevashi. This runs right up to the women who resisted majoritarian violence in their efforts to break the taboo on the entry of women of menstruating ages at the forest shrine of Sabarimala in recent years. I am convinced now that streevashi must be claimed as a value and practice by Indian feminism, as referring to a 'kind of inner empowerment that leads women to perform critical acts, rather than just be part of critical mass, and to perform them doggedly, ignoring all sorts of patriarchal violence and advice, until the power gives way', as I have argued elsewhere.[1]

In other words, I no longer trace the genealogy of feminism in Kerala primarily to the women whose writings feature in this volume. However, there can be no denying the fact that they belong within it, and we must indeed turn to them to both build on and dismantle their legacies. I have learned much about them since 2004. For example, I have come across inspiring accounts of the struggle the first generation feminist women engaged in to enter modern education and employment, some of which qualify to be streevashi and are spread over three whole generations. There are accounts of how the first generation of modern-educated women supported each other, building enduring ties of friendship. They helped each other to tide over great challenges in their personal lives, found each other opportunities for employment and education, and helped each other to settle down in new places of work outside Kerala. I have unearthed more and more evidence for the sidelining of this generation: so much so that information about some of them seems to be retrievable only from the biographies of their husbands who were well-known public figures of their times (for example, about Nidheerikal Mariam or Mrs. I. C. Chacko, from the biography of her husband; Elizabeth Kuruvila, from the biography of her husband K. K. Kuruvila). I have noticed how the most intellectually-oriented of them who also had the resources almost inevitably migrated outside Kerala and built interesting lives for themselves. For example, the mathematician T. A. Sarasvati Amma, A. C. Janakiamma, A. C. Devakiamma, the botanist E. K. Janaki Ammal and others.

It is true that feminists in Kerala have actively taken apart much of the imagination of gender that the first generation feminists worked with, but in this volume we preserve a part that we cannot do without, especially in the difficult times in which we live. Indeed, the difference between the feminist public voice in Kerala and that of the Hindutva women was flagrantly evident during the Shudra riots around women's entry into the Sabarimala of 2018–19.[2] The feminist voice was essentially a continuation of the collective voice that emerges from this volume, and it wielded all the intellectual tools of modernity: critical thinking, observation, humour. In contrast, the Hindutva women seemed to reject the very idea of an independent voice, pointing, rather, to the professed power of their *shaapam,* the curse, which, they claim, mobilizes the power that ostensibly accrues to them from years of living Hindu-womanly lives of piety and obedience.

All the more reason, then, to thank Sage-Stree for taking the initiative to reprint the book. I have been truly grateful to them for having seen the value of such a collection at a time the Malayalam publishing world had rejected it, refusing to even believe that women could write like this. We have come a long way from then, and the first edition of this volume has contributed its bit to the journey. I am sure that its second appearance, too, will offer much to think of.

Centre for Development Studies J. Devika
Thiruvananthapuram.

Notes

1. J. Devika, 'The Triumph of Streevaashi: Women Break the Wall of Caste at Sabarimala', 2 Jan. 2019, *Kafila,* https://kafila.online/2019/01/02/the-triumph-of-streevasashi-women-break-the-wall-of-caste-at-sabarimala/ [accessed on 11 Feb. 2021]
2. Otherwise known as 'Nairs'. In Kerala, the Shudras share upper caste privileges and were the chief force backing the Hindutva forces locally.

Acknowledgements

So many loving hands have by now helped me to craft this work that I have quite lost all unhealthy sense of possessiveness about it. Most of these articles were collected as a part of my research into gender and individualization in early modern Kerala. Then a senior researcher and friend, N. K. Raveendran, gave me a marvelous gift: his entire collection of articles from Malayalam magazines of the same period. Ten of the articles in this volume have been picked out of his collection. Every bit of the wonderful excitement of coming across such a rich archive was shared with Dr. T. K. A. Neesar and Dr. P. J. Cheriyan saw the relevance of publishing it earlier than anyone else. A great many friends and teachers helped me to locate articles, find the biographical details of authors and to trim and polish the translations: this is as much their book as it is mine. I would like to mention especially Govindan Nair at the Ulloor Smaraka Grandhasala, Thiruvananthapuram, K. C. Narayanan, Dr. M. Gangadharan, T. K. Anandi, Dr. A. Gopalankutty, Roshni Vijayan, L. Unnikrishnan, K. M. Seeti, K. O. Shamsuddin, G. Priyadarshan, Dilip Raj, Dr. N. A. Karim, Prema N. Nair, Prema Nair, Pramod Nair, Dr. M. R. Raghava Varier, Udaya Kumar, Anoop Madhavan, Radhakrishnan Channar, Muttattu Bhaskaran Channar, Thankam Ramachandran, Muralidharan, P. Ramkumar, Niaz, Sreedevi K. Nayar, Krishnakumar, K.M. Ashraf, Reshmi, Susmita, and M. K. Leela. Others have sustained me through an extremely taxing spell: Praveena, Ruchi, Judith, Bobby, Sreedevi, Usha Zacharias, Beena, Gilbert, Anindita, Mary, Rati, Narayanan and Shahjahan, Paul Zacharia's ideas for the title and Gauri's ideas for the cover are gratefully acknowledged.

At home, the excitement was infectious. My little girls, like all little girls, were only too ready to be pulled into a pleasant thrill, though they had no clue as to why I should be so elated over ladies of long ago. Sreekutty, however, fussed about me at times like a protective mother hen, suggesting that I should not pine away for information, in her words, 'about A. Kalyani Amma or B. Amma', was patient, supportive and cheerful, despite a number of hazards because of me since I couldn't stop twittering on and on about my work, to massive telephone bills. But towards the end, even she caught the fever, and was meditating on how we could trace out some author who refused to appear. I managed to pass on the giddiness to my parents and Radhachittamma, and even drag my sister in to read the drafts; they were glad to see me so happy, and supported me in all possible ways. I only hope all of them will find this book enjoyable, and worth all the trouble.

Introduction

Writing to C. W. E. Cotton, Agent to the Governor of Madras in response to his inquiries regarding a certain Lakshmikutty Amma from Tiruvitamkoor (Travancore), M. E. Watts, the Dewan of Tiruvitamkoor remarked: 'This clever young Nair lady has got on by her own efforts. She is headstrong, mannish and full of the perfervid spirit that espouses lost causes.' The young lady in question was the daughter of a retired senior official in the Tiruvitamkoor Education Department, and had taught at Queen Mary's College, Madras, before she proceeded on leave to London for studies in 1926. There she is said to have completed studies in a year and then set off all by herself on a tour of Europe, with the help of friends, she claimed. Watts observed that Lakshmikutty had made friends with K. M. Panikkar and the 'Strickland crowd', and her antecedents made her rather suspect. Watts had been informed that early in the 1920s, as a schoolteacher in Thiruvananthapuram, she was deeply interested in Gandhi and non-cooperation, and even tried to popularize these subjects among her pupils. He, however, remarked that now she was on her way back to Thiruvananthapuram, the best place to cool her ardour.[1]

The picture of Lakshmikutty Amma, which emerges from this official correspondence, matches almost exactly with the caricature of the 'speech-making woman' etched by the well-known Malayali humourist Sanjayan in the 1930s.[2] This figure, too, is stridently assertive, eager to take the stage against male dominance at the slightest provocation, 'mannish' to say the least and in the last reckoning, pretty harmless. For all her tumult, she evokes but a few tremors, which turn out to be not as dreadful as these may have seemed.

This was how the first generation of Malayali feminists was represented in their heyday, by writers located in very different fields of Malayali society in the late 1920s and 1930s, only to be wiped out of collective memory a few decades hence. Though not all of them were authors, many engaged with the emergent public sphere in early twentieth-century Kerala on behalf of a collectivity of 'Women', assuming that all women had in common certain interests, inclinations, which made them important to society, and certain rights, which society had to concede. Of course, some were remembered, with a curious sifting powerfully in place. Anna Chandy, for instance, continued to be remembered, not as a powerful feminist intellectual, which she indeed was, but as a 'woman-achiever'; Lalithambika Antharjanam continues to be much lauded not for her powerful critique of individualizing modern gender, and her feminist reconstruction of it, but as the epitome of a very non-disruptive Motherliness. Some, of course, were almost entirely erased: B. Bhageeraty Amma, who had edited for twenty years what may arguably be called one of the leading magazines for women in early twentieth-century Kerala, and was an acclaimed public speaker of those times, is little remembered. The articles collected here were all published between the 1890s, when these women began to air their views in the emergent Malayali public sphere, and the late 1930s, after which they go into an odd decline, yet to be fully explained.

However, I would not like to present these authors as a brave generation that lost out against modern patriarchy, as a prominent author has.[3] The fact that they stayed well-within the framework of modern gender as it was presented in Malayali society of the late nineteenth and early twentieth centuries, committed to the goal of sexual complementarity it promised, can hardly be overlooked. By 'modern gender', one would mean *(a)* the presupposition of the division of the world into 'public' and 'private' domains, appropriate for men and women respectively, who are seen to possess distinctly sexed 'dispositions' that direct them to the spaces deemed right for them; *(b)* compulsory heterosexism; *(c)* a strong claim to represent the 'natural' foundations of human social order, with the cautionary rider that for this 'natural' aspect of humanity to manifest in society, a great deal of social activity, ranging from legal interventions to training through modern education, is necessary. The established *Jati*-based social ordering in Kerala, which valued *Janma-bhedam*, or difference in birth, came to be repeatedly denounced in the late nineteenth century, from a range of sites, including the missionaries, and the newly educated elite. In these denunciations, an alternative was posed, often implicitly. This is what I would like to call 'the order of gender', an ideal form of social ordering projected into the future (and re-discovered in the 'past' as well, in the imaginings of the 'Golden Ages' of, for example, Indian/Hindu society), in which the only unsurpassable social division would be of gender. The division between men and women also implied two distinct social domains deemed 'naturally-ordained' for them, the public and the domestic. The 'order of gender' was to be sustained through the complementary exchange of gendered capacities, men as industrious producers in the political, economic and intellectual fields, and women as efficient and active overseers of the domestic domain. While material sorts of authority was largely assigned as male, a certain sentimental and moral authority, that was to work not through force and violence but by the gentle power of persuasion, of words, was designated Womanly. Modern education, then, was set the task of 'developing' the 'natural' (gendered) capacities inherent in specific bodies to shape internalities that would help the modern Individual, the product of such training, to conform to idealized modern gendered subjectivities. The Individual, thus believed to be culled out of the traditional order and shaped through modern institutions, or in another language, 'freed from bondage to tradition', was always and already implicated in a modern collectivity. Modern gender was to mediate this implication crucially.

To my mind, the political significance of the writers of these essays collected here lies in two important claims they persistently made. First, it was asserted that women, by Nature, deserved to have a thoroughly active supervisory role within the home not as passive domestic labourers but as active agents overseeing not only the materials but also the souls within the home. Woman as the guardian of the home and hearth was to exist in a relation of complementarity with Man, whose proper domain was deemed to be the public, within the spheres of political power, wealth-creation and intellectual production. By the late 1920s, this argument had gained significant diffusion in the Malayali public sphere, enthusiastically taken up by almost all the community reform movements in Tiruvitamkoor, Kochi (Cochin) and Malabar. Many of the first-generation feminists were active propagators of this new active domestic ideal for women (for instance, Ayesha Mayan and K. Chinnamma, both in this volume). By the 1920s and 1930s the new domestic ideal was also refurbished by the inclusion of moneymaking activities, such as cottage industry, minor farming, animal husbandry and so on (see the articles by Pennammabhayi and Konniyoor Meenakshi Amma in this volume). Secondly, by the late 1920s, many of these women-intellectuals claimed that the boundaries that separated the modern home from the world outside were becoming increasingly blurred (V. K. Chinnammalu Amma's article in this volume is certainly an interesting sample of this argument). Earlier, the modern home was envisaged as a site that worked best with the power of 'gentle words, emotions, prayers, devotion and tears'; it appeared most obviously to be the space of Woman, who seemed naturally equipped to exercise such power. Now, however, with an increasing number of institutions seeking to rely upon such power, rather than upon the use of physical violence—such as schools, hospitals, philanthropic institutions, local bodies—it was argued that women's 'special capacities' had a relevance outside the home. Thus it could be argued that the Womanly might no longer be identified with a certain space, but with a certain form of power. Many first generation feminists based their arguments in favour of paid employment for women outside the home, on this claim. Thus they were hardly asking for unconditional freedom of life-choices for women; with rare exceptions, they were demanding an expansion of women's space without challenging the claims regarding the 'quintessential qualities of Womanliness'.

Moreover, this second claim was not necessarily made *against* the first. K. Chinnamma's article in this volume perhaps illustrates well how a woman who had herself entered much larger social concerns ardently espoused the ideal of a taxing modern domesticity which demanded eternal vigilance over children from women and women alone. These were determined efforts to carve a specifically 'Woman's domain' that straddled the domestic and (ever-expanding) parts of the public, in various fields ranging from politics to literature, without jeopardising a certain hallowed Womanliness. Two articles in this volume, one by K. M. Kunhulakshmy Kettilamma and the other by B. Bhageeraty Amma, illustrate well how the case for women's active presence in the literary field was built upon a claim regarding their 'intrinsic nature' (the latter article mobilises not only Nature but also History). Forceful arguments in favour of recognizing women as a group with distinct political interests were also made in the late 1920s (the editorial of the *Vanitakusumam* in this collection is a good example of such strong appeals), very often, coupled with their 'special' significance.

The flip side was of course the idea that women needed to be more self-disciplined, industrious and responsible than men. This followed on the heels of the idea that women were natural disciplinarians, and hence were the custodians of social order and morality. Throughout the late nineteenth and early twentieth centuries, reflections on building a new 'modern' self had insisted upon a distinction between *swatantryam* ('self-means for survival') and *tantonnittam* (doing-as-one-pleased). The former was valued, the latter condemned, and these were linked in a binary relation. Swatantryam meant also the capacity to conform to ideal modern gendered subjectivities, to 'attain' Womanhood or Manhood, and did not mean the simple absence of all forms of coercion. It would not be off the mark to claim that through all these decades, educated Malayalis have got used to identifying 'freedom' with an active agency which is economically productive and congenial to the interests of, mainly, the family. This has been especially so for women, for whatever attempts to challenge this and redefine freedom have hardly been attentive to the gender divide. One has to merely refer to the representations of 'women's progress' in the 'Kerala Model' literature to see how this idea has remained unchallenged within academics: indeed it remains one of the most powerful props to the 'Kerala Model' itself. It is certainly true that these women intellectuals had to engage in prolonged and charged debate with modern men in the public sphere and were often marginalised as unrealistic rabble-rousers. However, the extent of their differences with male reformers should not be exaggerated. In fact, many of these authors assiduously pointed out that their intention was not to abandon Womanliness (by, for instance, taking jobs in the police or excise), and were at pains to establish that no revolution was to be feared. Further, some were quite willing to condemn and put down a revolution, if it did break out as an unintended consequence.

This however, is not to belittle the political significance of this writing. One would have to be blind not to see the political significance of Anna Chandy's hard-hitting attack (in this volume) on T. K. Velu Pillai. Here was a 24-year-old Syrian Christian woman, barely out of Law School, literally barging into a public meeting in Thiruvananthapuram, presided over by a revered (male) judge and scholar, demanding that they hear her 'defence' of employment for married women, and unleashing a formidable attack on a Nair intellectual, a Professor of Law, twice her age, and a political and intellectual heavyweight in Tiruvitamkoor. Much of this writing effectively blocks efforts to whine over the contamination of a constructed 'inner-space'. This was imagined as a pristine core of culture, which women seemed to embody, as distinct from an 'outer' or 'public' space contaminated by things foreign, often by noted male intellectuals of those times. Many of the articles in this collection are rejoinders or polemical responses to often highly placed or distinguished male intellectuals, for instance, those by N. A. Amma, B. Pachi Amma, Mrs. K. Kannan Menon, and C. P. Kalyani Amma and others. Or they were directed against prevailing ideas, entrenched prejudices in the public sphere. Thus E. Narayanikutty Amma's article in this collection tries to circumvent the restriction imposed by the editor of the journal she was writing in that women should not get tangled in political issues; Parvaty Ayyappan's note criticises the adulation of Mussolini's passive and home-bound wife as model for wifehood; Tottaikkattu Madhavi Amma writes against a flippant misrepresentation of her conduct as legislator in the Cochin Legislative Council. Nor do I wish to obscure the 'internal fractures' in the adulation of active domesticity. Mrs. I. C. Chacko's speech in this volume, though staying well within the advocacy of active domesticity, I am certain, would have given the jitters not only to the orthodox, but even to the champions of modern domesticity for women. Such is its insistence on the home as not just the space of Woman's labours, but also of her comfort, and unabashed support of pleasure, which look dangerously close to 'excessive self-indulgence'!

As someone who grew up seeing political/intellectual docility as a necessary requirement for coming under the sign of Woman in Kerala, I was awestruck by the marvellous deployment of reason, humour and rhetoric in these writings (many of which were actually speeches) to dismantle older forms of patriarchy, even to ferret out what appeared to be the vestiges of it in emergent institutions (for instance, Parvati Nenminimangalam, in this volume). Nor were they blind to emergent advantages to men, shaped often within reformism that claimed to liberate women; K. PadmavatyAmma's criticism of the spread of dowry (in this volume) among the Nairs reveals this well. The quickness and the dexterity with which the intellectual tools available to the modern-educated were seized and pressed into the service of the imagined collectivity of Women (i.e. something that came into being at the sites of its strategic political invocation) is something I hope this collection will convey. Anna Chandy's brilliant use of legal discourse is one excellent instance. The strategies deployed in this disarming really deserve detailed treatment. Along with efforts to de-mystify the place of women in the traditional home by pointing out its limitedness and the distressing restraints it imposed (Pachi Amma, for example) and even to reject it outright (see Anna Chandy's polemic against domestic labour), there were attempts to reclaim the kitchen, to make it a space of social emancipation and transformation (Devaki Narikkattiri, in this volume). A common strategy is to plumb a given text for its internal contradictions and omissions, acknowledged or unacknowledged, and to lay bare the interests underlying it as those of patently non-modern male dominance. The article titled 'Womanliness', signed by 'Sarojini', which is a formidable denunciation of the instability of the notion of Womanliness in the pedagogic efforts of educated men to improve women, provides as excellent instance of such precise and merciless dissection (also see K. Lakshmi Amma, in this volume). Another familiar strategy is to point to developments in the Western world, especially those in the women's movements there, to argue for active social agency for women here, for example, in K. Mary Thomas's short article in the present collection. There is also an interesting attempt to draw indirectly upon theories from anthropology and psychology to explain male dominance as a universal phenomenon, an effort that had woefully few successors in Kerala (Kochattil Kalyanikutty Amma, in this collection). If I have any cause for regret about this work, it is surely about my inability to include in it some of Lalithambika Antharjanam's short stories, for example *Prateekshakal* (1936–37).[4] Antharjanam's uniqueness was certainly her skilled use of modern literary genres to intervene in the discourse of modern gendering, her remarkable critique of the individualisation effected by modern gendering and of the non-reversible relations of power between the Reformer-Male and the woman he reformed, found necessary in many versions of social reformism. *Prateekshakal* is perhaps, the most damning statement I have found about Reformer Man's shaping of the woman's mind and life, a theme familiar to Malayalis ever since O. Chandu Menon's acclaimed novel, *Indulekha* (1889), and repeated endlessly within Malayala Brahmin reformism of the 1930s.

Thus even as I maintained a conscious wariness against setting up intellectual fore-mothers, I could not help listening enraptured to the 'fantasy-echo' so aptly named by the historian Joan W. Scott in her attempt to understand how feminists of different generations, with often diametrically-opposed concerns, are able to 'connect'.[5] As translator, I found myself grappling with several new ideas: many of these writers had indeed 'named' forms of gender oppression rampant in the Malayali society I grew up in, for which I had no name. The most telling instance was Anna Chandy's coinage *Adukkalavadam*, which translates as 'Kitchenism', which refers to the belief that women's legitimate space, all said and done, is indeed the space of domestic labour.

Yet it is crucially important to see what is excluded from the Womanhood that is imagined in these writings. The elitism inherent in much of this writing is something I would not like to conceal at all: racism and even a pathological concern over blue blood, is often present, even if in an oblique way. Indeed, even as the Womanly domain was being opened up and widened at tremendous effort, it immediately created other spaces that were 'non-Womanly'. For instance, the nominated representative of women in the Cochin Legislative Council was vociferously arguing in 1929 that women should be prohibited from the production and sale of liquor.[6] Women who were far removed from modern education, women of the labouring classes and less-privileged groups are present in these writings only as junior members at best, as aspirants for full membership in Womanhood, who had to be guided into it under the tutelage of women with adequate cultural capital. A recent study of the constitution of the female workforce in the cashew industry in Kerala reveals the extent to which the women of the poorer classes with little access to modern education were separated from the first-generation feminists.[7] For them, modern gender began to shape everyday life not so much through their heightened exposure to new ideals and aspirations, as through governmental interventions in wage-fixing. However, one of the pieces in this volume is an appeal to the 'Hindu Women of Kerala', actually, to the *savarna* women, asking them to join the Vaikom Satyagraha against the restrictions of movement imposed on the lower castes in the roads around the Vaikom temple, to help alleviate the disabilities of their lower-caste sisters (Vatakkecharuvil P. K. Kalyani). In her attack on T. K. Velu Pillai, Anna Chandy questions his reduction of all Malayali women to those of the matrilineal castes, and presents an alternate construction, of a Malayali Womanhood separated by caste differences, but united by the common experience of oppressive traditional restrictions and mistreatment. That, perhaps, indicates the limits of the inclusiveness of Womanhood as conceived by the first generation feminists, remaining as it was within the ambit of modern gender that presupposed the public-private divide as expressing a gendered delineation of social space.

One of the most interesting pieces in the present set of writings is a brief note signed by Ittichiriyamma, on the issue of married women taking on their husbands' names. It is evident that this certainly does not sit comfortably among texts that express passionate convictions in favour of monogamous (monoandrous?) marriage; indeed, many articles collected here are of that persuasion. The (rather unsuccessful) effort made to amalgamate the female agency within matriliny and the ideal of the modern homemaker is also interesting in that the distance between the two is rendered all the more conspicuous. But the most heart-warming of all the writings presented here is the short account given by Mantaraveetil Lakshmy Amma, of her 'life and home-making', written in 1906–07. I only hope my ungraceful words manage to convey at least some part of the charmingly un-self-conscious liveliness with which this happy young woman spoke to me about her *taravad* (homestead), *karanavan* (male head of the matrilineal household), husband, and daily routine, from across nearly a century! Besides being a lovely text, it is a historian's delight, exhibiting in every sentence the complexity of the transition to modernity. None of the stereotypes of the late nineteenth-century Malayalam 'Nair' novels appears here: the restrictive taravad, the villainous karanavan and so on. Lakshmy Amma adores her taravad, her karanavan, and her husband who does not have much modern education, precisely because they seem to embody the modern ideals of self-discipline, frugality, dignity of the individual and labour. She gently scoffs at established and emergent ways in which fairly well-to-do Nairs sought social mobility, and locates her 'advancement' solely in that made possible by a life of labour, prudence and self-discipline and above all, the ability to choose those elements from whatever was being paraded as 'modern'. And for me, the most inspiring image evoked by these writings is that of eighteen-year-old M. Haleema Beevi addressing an audience of about two hundred women at a conference she had organized in 1938. She spoke of the 'large heartedness' inherent in education, reminding her audience that this has made it possible for severely-restricted women to come together to assert their self-respect (M. Haleema Beevi, this collection). For a Malayali woman like me who lives and works in today's Kerala where education for women is nothing but a means for upward mobility of the family, this could not be but inspiring.

Any translation is also an act of appropriation; my rendering of these writings into a different language is certainly mediated by the theoretical-political lenses that make them intelligible to me. Yet, I was also constantly alert to those moments in which these writings moved away from the familiar, or when the familiar itself seemed redone, turned unfamiliar. As for the criterion of selection, the idea was to bring in as wide a discussion as possible, to convey the sheer sweep and intensity of the debate about modern gender and its implications for women. I also searched hard for voices from all social groups. However, this was a demand hard to satisfy and the reader will notice that a large number of these voices do represent the newly educated elite that emerged dominant in and through the upheavals of the late nineteenth and early twentieth century in Malayali society.

Lastly, though a certain hypochondria regarding authors has largely spared me, there is some reason to raise the vexed question of authorship in this context. My search for biographical details of these writers is a story in itself. Many of these writers proved, quite expectedly, to be mothers, wives and sisters of very famous men of the period. I do believe that these women never attained their moment in the sun purely and simply because they conformed to the gendered division that has always characterized the Malayali public sphere: women write of 'Womanly' matters; men discuss 'general' issues. However, I have been unable to trace out the biographical details of all, and there is a further possibility. The despicable habit of writing under female names, passing off radical opinions under that mask, was common enough even among much adored reformers in early twentieth century Kerala (a malady that seems to be resurfacing lately).[8] Many who saw this material were so impressed by it that they immediately concluded that it must have been some men writing under women's names. Though I do protest against their attitude, I am willing to concede that it is quite possible that some of the authors were not women at all. Nevertheless, I remain undeterred. For instance, I am quite prepared to accept that 'Mantaraveetil Lakshmy Amma', the writer of one of my favourite pieces, whom I was unable to trace out, could well have been just a fabricated name! In fact, one could argue that this realization serves as a salutary corrective to some of the excesses that feminist history is now outgrowing. The idea that historical rootedness is necessary for the stability of the subject of feminism is not as convincing now as it used to be. What makes these texts interesting ultimately is not so much the femaleness of their authors, as the fact that they all make appeals to, speak on behalf of, espouse a politics allegedly of 'Women' as a distinct group, with recognizable commonness of inclination, interests, and rights. To highlight this, I have included in the set an article signed rather ambiguously as 'KPM'. Nor will I heed the sensible counsel to 'stay on the safe side' by sticking to slightly-better known authors like B. Kalyani Amma, Ambady Karthyayani Amma, Taravath Ammalu Amma, and so on. In any case, my purpose is certainly not to discover matchless and indefatigable Joan of Arcs, infallible do-gooders in the past, as has been amply indicated in the previous pages. As a beleaguered woman researcher in early twenty-first century Malayali society, I do catch the strains of a distant 'fantasy-echo', but I will not let that lull me into a depoliticised and irresponsible somnolence.

Notes

1 M. E. Watts to C. W. E. Cotton, 13 January 1928, 317/ 877, Bundle No. 18, *Confidential Files*, Tiruvitamkoor, Kerala State Archives. The young lady in question did not cool her heels, really. She became well known later as Lakshmi N. Menon, Parliament Secretary to the Prime Minister of India from 1952–57, and Minister in the Foreign Affairs Department from 1957–66.
2 Sanjayan (M. R. Nair), 'Sreemati Taravath Ammalu Amma—Oru Anusmaranam' (Taravath Ammalu Amma—A Remembrance) in Sanjayan 1970: 163–64.
3 K. Saradamoni, 1999: 116–45. Another work that has made extensive use of these writings is Raveendran 1992.
4 From Antharjanam, 1952.
5 Joan W. Scott 2001: 284–306.
6 *Malayala Manorama*, 4 August 1928.
7 Anna Lindberg, 2001.
8 The notorious setting up of a 'Vanneri Savitri Antharjanam' with radical opinions by two prominent Malayala Brahmin reformers in the 1930s, and the harm it did to the credibility of women's self-expression in the Nambutiri reform movement is quite well known. But much before, representing oneself as female or under female pseudonyms was known. In the *Mitavadi*, for instance, names like 'Oru Vishishta Stree' (A Genteel Woman) and 'Oru Purushan' (A Man) were adopted by opponents in debates about culture and religion, and which invariably touched upon questions of gender. See G. Priyadarshan, 1982: 121–22.

1
N. A. Amma

Unfortunately, there is no information available about this author.

The Demerits of Female Education: A Refutation

Readers of the *Vidyavinodini* have probably read the article titled 'Streevidyabhyasam' (Female Education) written by a respectable gentleman in the *Vrishchikam* [Nov–Dec] issue.[1] In my perception and faith, there are very few of us who cannot read and write. So also, many women and men still possess considerable skill in both poetry and prose; but no one has responded to that article. I wish to offer a few words, deeply grieved and surprised by such neglect.

(i) The first point made [in that article] is that 'knowledge by means of letters is seen to be of little use to women'. A scholar has remarked that 'a man without learning may be taken to be but some sort of beast'. Our experience shows that this is indeed true. All education requires the knowledge of the letters in a crucial way. It is doubtful whether any other form of education is as useful. With appropriate training, all the necessary human qualities are acquired in such education. The truth of this contention is well illustrated by the life histories of figures such as Melpattur Narayana Bhattatiri, the author of *Narayaneeyam*.[2] In his youth, Bhattatiri was an ignorant oaf. It was his education in letters that made him world-renowned later in life. Thus it is evident that learning through letters is indeed crucial in elevating the feeble-minded into highly intelligent and distinguished personages. The greatness of a literate education is truly beyond words. Therefore it must never be argued that a literate education, which holds manifold advantages, is necessary for some, but not for others.

(ii) 'Literacy is useful only in managing political affairs' is the next point. This is wholly erroneous. Most people in our lands are literate. At least one-half of them have nothing to do with politics in living their lives. To this day, literacy is regarded to be useful to a person, to others, in this world, and in the next. Perhaps it is his ignorance of women who have ruled the world then and now, like Queen Elizabeth, that prompts this man to recommend that 'women must never be entrusted with political affairs'. It is quite well known that few kings have rivalled Elizabeth and Queen Victoria as rulers of England. Nevertheless, if men have indeed acquired the birthright to run political affairs, as this gentleman has decided, let it be so. Are women allowed to manage at least domestic affairs? The appellative *grhini* applies to the woman who runs the home. To run domestic affairs, a certain level of intelligence and education are necessary. The good and evil of humankind arise from the ways in which homes are managed. Good and bad qualities take root in young children while they are under the care of their mother.

'The habits of a tender age, will they be forgotten, ever'[3]— true, indeed. Therefore, women need literacy even to run domestic matters. A third argument put forth is that 'because some amount of their blood flows out uncontrollably, women are weak'. The blood that flows out thus is impure; according to the science of the body, many diseases will follow if such discharge does not take place. Indeed, such regular discharge makes the body healthy, and enlarges the mind. 'With education, women will lose the modesty that is their ornament, and get obsessed with adultery and other evils', indeed! If education creates evils like adultery, though the lack of modesty may not generate any evil [in men], does that mean that adultery and other vices are beneficial to men [for whom the letters seem appropriate]? If someone commits an evil deed, people call him unenlightened. Education is necessary to remove such ignorance. Therefore, there can be no link between education and adultery and other such lechery. My knowledge is that education eradicates such evil.

The aforementioned author draws evidence from the *Sakuntalam* to prove that ancient women like Sakunatala were illiterate: he claims that her words in the Third Act of the *Sakuntalam* were merely inserted to perfect the narrative, and that in the Fourth Act, Kanva advises Sakuntala not through writing, but through speech. How can this be correct? In the First Act, when Sakuntala and her companions speak with the king, he notices their astonished glances at seeing the letters carved in the royal seal on his ring. He assures them that it was indeed received from the king. This proves that not only Sakuntala but also her companions were literate. Kanva gives her verbal advice not because she was illiterate, or knew nothing of Chaste Wifehood. When a person climbs a tree, another person standing beneath may caution him to hold on fast. However, this is not because the climber is unaware of the need to grip well. It is normal practice to offer such caution. Kanva's advice, too, was in that spirit. Besides, can it be not the case that Kanva's words were inserted for perfecting the narrative, in the same way as it is being argued regarding Sakuntala's words?

A woman scholar made it possible for the author of *Sakuntalam* to assume the name of 'Kalidasa'. She had vowed to marry only a scholar who could defeat her in debate; resentful scholars who had failed the test manipulated her into marrying an ignorant goatherd. Everyone knows the rest of the story, according to which, this lady sent him off with sound advice to the temple of Goddess Kali, and at the end of which he became a great scholar, and remains, to this day, the crown jewel of scholars. Therefore it is proven that there were women scholars in ancient times. It is said that in ancient Aryavarta, women could read and write; that four hundred years before the Age of the Epics, women held positions of dignity; that they were not prohibited from walking on the main roads, attending large meetings, and participating in political affairs. In *Uttararamacharita*, Atreyi tells the Goddess of the Forest about her study of the Upanishads with Valmiki. From this it seems clear that women of these those times did persevere in such endeavours. Many more examples can be cited. That can be reserved for another occasion.

I do not forget that the impartial authors of articles titled 'Vyabhicharasamanyam', 'Malayala Streekal', and 'Swabhavavum Dharanasaktiyum', which appeared in *Vidyavinodini* in the years 1068 [1892–93], 1069 [1893–94] and 1070 [1894–95],[4] have sufficiently described Womanly virtues, and included literacy among them. Though God has differentiated women and men into two distinct groups, they have been granted equal levels of intelligence. Education is unavoidable if that intelligence is to evolve. An education that seeks to broaden the mind cannot do without literacy. The benefits to be reaped through the acquisition of literacy by all women and men are wonderful. Literacy serves us in this world and the next, in worldly concerns and in spiritual salvation. Much more may be written about knowledge, but the limitation of space impels me to close my words.

From 'Streevidyabhyasa Doshanishedham', *Vidyavinodini* 8, 11, Malayalam Era, henceforth ME, 1073 Chingam (Aug-Sept 1897): 427–31.

Notes

1 Refers to article signed 'N.R.V', titled 'Streevidyabhyasam', *Vidyavinodini*, 8, 2, 1896: 73–77, which divided education into three types: to be obtained verbally through advice and sermons; through learning letters; and by practical training in crafts and other activity. The author argued that only the first and third suited women, and that learning letters was not only useless, but also actually the source of much harm to them.

2 Melapattur Narayana Bhattatiri was the famous poet and grammarian of medieval Kerala associated with the court of the Zamorin (*samutiri*) of Calicut (Kozhikode). He is recognized as the author of *Prakriyasarvaswam, Ashtamichampu, Narayaneeyam* and many other works.

3 '*Cheruppakalangalilulla Sheelam/Marakkumo Manushanulla Kalam.*'

4 The Malayalam calendar follows the Kollam Era, which began in A.D. 825. It is a lunar calendar of 12 months, and the Malayalam year begins in mid-August of the Gregorian calendar. So, Malayalam months are usually spread over two months of the Gregorian calendar : for instance, the month of Chingam would be August-September. Also, the Malayalam year does not exactly match the Gregorian year because it runs from mid-August to mid-August. Publications that appear in the month of Dhanu of the Malayalam calendar actually fall between two Gregorian years, i.e., the December of one year and the January of the next.

2
K. Lakshmy Amma

There is no fully reliable information about this author, but some have suggested, convincingly to my mind, that this could have been K. Lakshmy Amma who was one of the earliest woman officers in the Travancore (Tiruvitamkoor) Education Department. She entered Travancore government service in the first decade of the twentieth century, as Assistant Inspectress of Schools, and a close associate of B. Kalyani Amma, one of the editors of the journal Sharada, *in which this article appears. She is also said to have been associated with Nair reformism, particularly with the Nair Service Society, and was a speaker in many NSS annual conferences.*

Manly Duty

A number of articles propounding various sorts of duties like Wifely Duty, Womanly Duty, and so on, are frequently seen these days; I have often wondered why nothing is being published on the Duty of Husbands, or Manly Duty, likewise. Is it that only women are unmindful of their duties? On the other hand, is it that men have no responsibilities? Such qualms do arise. The responsibilities to be borne by men and women are almost equal. It cannot be said that one party has more, or less, than the other does.

There is a Greek legend about the ancient times in which human beings had four arms, four legs and two faces. The Gods, bitten with envy for these powerful creatures, split them in two, into Man and Woman. Although this tale is not credible, the Hindu percept that 'the wife is half the man' does pay some obeisance to it. If this is so, no difference should be envisioned between Woman and Man. There is no doubt that if caring for the husband is the duty of the wife, then caring for the wife is certainly the duty of the husband. Marriage occupies a crucial place in human life.

Woman is not merely a child-producing machine. The worldly-wise are well aware that men are the source of the suffering that women, by nature delicate and susceptible to the rigours of age, endure. The widower is free to remarry, but not so the widow! The saying that the 'sorrow of the loss of a wife is remedied by taking another'[1] reflects how shallow the emotional ties to a wife are. If it were a woman who said this, it would be readily rejected as the fruit of ignorance. This is definitely a man's machination! It was also a man who declared that 'Woman does not deserve freedom'.[2] The [British] Prime Minister who said he had not even the time to see the Englishwoman who had gone to him to plead for female representation in Parliament, he too, is a man. In this discussion, the comment made by the famous Mr. W. T. Stead is very interesting.[3] He said that the ingratitude of the men of England, who have forgotten their mothers in their various efforts to achieve power and freedom, is quite astonishing.

Only gracious and gentle womenfolk will tolerate the great offences done to them by innumerable lawmakers. The efforts of illustrious figures to promote widow remarriage are thwarted by the natural conservatism of many who are said to be respectable members of the community! Marriage is generally looked upon as an auspicious occasion for men. Conjugal bliss prompts Man to pursue various kinds of enterprise diligently. It also helps to prevent him from wandering afar from morality. About those servants of the world who proclaim marriage to be the root of sorrow, the least said, the better. These friends are capable only of lamenting the negative sides of worldly affairs. The world can only grieve about them; there is little to congratulate in their attitude. We need not forget the blessings and virtues of marriage. All the joys of marriage emanate from the wife. [But] If the wife must be sweet-tempered, the husband should also be amiable to her. As in Nature in which all forces act upon each other, so also amongst human beings, emotions act upon each other. Men should necessarily be attentive towards women who respect their husbands and diligently serve them, no matter how much they may suffer in their hands. There is little doubt that those who do not heed the light of this recognition are cads. If that Great Soul who advised a virtuous woman 'not to hurt one's co-wife, even when hurt by her'[4] had also advised Man not to 'hurt' one's wife, then the sorrows of Sakuntala would not have scorched the minds of readers. Is it because no one insists upon Manly Duty that Mankind remains utterly ungrateful to Womankind, who toil all the time for the comfort of their husbands, disregarding their own distress? Does anyone revere Ugratapas, the husband of Seelavathi?[5] Can Man expect lenience from Woman, without showing it to her? Is it not usually the case that the husband who calls his wife 'wicked' turns out to be the vile one? Is it not proper that Man, who feels the need for freedom, should also feel it necessary to grant it to Woman? Or, is Man's freedom merely a means of bolstering the slavery of Woman?

It is well known that variations of human character are caused by social contact. We tend to imitate people with whom we interact intimately. No matter how bad a woman's character may be while she still lives with her parents, it is not difficult for her to imitate her husband. The Woman's mind is simple and placid. A talented English poet has compared the female mind with a clear lake. Just as the lake turns turbulent and dirty when disturbed, amiable women will engender anguish and frustration when their minds are agitated. It is Man's inadequacy that brings about such a situation. Rarely do we hear of men accused of adultery, but the charge is frequently made against women. Adultery implies the transgression of established laws. The evils of adultery could not have emerged in society if the lawmakers had given some keen thought to the reason why women in their ignorance often violate the laws that have all been framed by men. Man's passion for self-gain is behind all such depravity. Therefore if women in any society turn subversive, we ought to blame the men. The great curse of humanity is that men, who ought to be alert towards the moral discipline of women in their capacity as fathers and husbands, are primarily interested in selfish gains. Therefore those Great Souls who would sermonize about Womanly Duty are well-advised to honour their obligations appropriately; if they do so, both parties will have no cause for complaint, and much to gain, besides.

From 'Purushadharmam', *Sharada* 1, 8, M.E. 1081 Mithunam (Jun–Jul 1906): 175–77.

Notes

1 *Bharyadukham Punarbharya.*
2 *Na Stree Swatantryamarhati.*
3 William T. Stead (1849–1912) was the editor of the *Pall Mall Gazette*, whose famous exposé of what came to be known as 'the white slave traffic' in London was widely reckoned as the most famous piece of scandal journalism in nineteenth-century England. He was an ardent sympathizer of the suffragist cause, and a good friend of Josephine Butler, Annie Besant and Millicent Garrett Fawcett.
4 The reference is the advice given to Sakuntala by her foster-father, the sage Kanva, as she was about to start her journey to the abode of her husband, King Dushyanta, in Kalidasa's *Sakuntalam.*
5 Ugratapas was a highly revered elderly sage, but ugly, ill tempered, diseased, nasty and debauched, and the husband of Seelavathi, young, beautiful and virtuous. Her extreme devotion to such a husband was so strong that she lived at his feet, ate only the remnants of his meal, totally effaced herself, and even carried him to the courtesan's house as was his wish. This was held up often as a model for *pativratayam*, or wifely devotion.

3

Manntaraveetil Lakshmy Amma

This author is not otherwise known. I have not been able to trace her, though she does provide some detail of her family and other whereabouts in this article.

An Account of My Life and My Homemaking

My ancestral home is in Vettatunad, in the Ponnani taluk of British Malabar. Though I was born in a matrilineal family, the system followed in my family since old times may be said to be somewhat like patriliny. In our family, women live with their husbands, usually, and only those who are unfortunate to lose them early return to live in their own homes.[1] Our taravad [joint family, also indicative of a common homestead] is endowed with all the rank and honour that a Nair family could possibly claim, and besides, we have properties that yield above 5000 rupees a year after all expenses. By the grace of God, our taravad is known in the locality never to have produced too many heirs with no virtue.

However, Nairs who do well enough to rise above poverty usually go crazy over jati-pride and rank, and decide that they will have none but Brahmins and kings for *sambandham*.[2] All the men and women are toiling in right earnest to become *ejamananmar* [landlords] and *netyarammamar* and *kunhammamar*, both titles indicate high status acquired through hypergamy, as wives of men of royal or aristocratic lineages), and making additions in deeds granting *kanam, pattam* or *panayam* [all different sorts of tenancies] to keezhdudiyanmar [under-tenants] that would indicate high rank and status—so that their positions as aristocrats or landlords are assured.[3] I would like to reveal, sorrowfully or happily, that not even an infant in our taravad has had the singular fortune of securing this easily attained and valuable source of wealth.

Besides, even the neighbours are aggrieved that merciless God has not blessed even a single lad in our family with a job of at least a guard in the *amsham* [a sub-division of a taluk], which would have been quite enough for him to be widely known as a lucky fellow! Furthermore, a scandal of a long duration that is still talked about is that members of the Manntara family whisper two mantras into the ears of their infants right on the day they are named: 'reduce your expenses' and 'increase your income'. Moreover, disapprobation of us for being buffoons who unnecessarily pour out money like water to educate their children, who would regardless have 'to clear the wild growth, till the land and scrub the pots' is not entirely absent. Whatever anyone might say, the women and men in our taravad have not yet abandoned the habit of scrubbing pots, cutting bushes and ploughing the land once they become adults.

On reaching the age of sixty, it is common for senior men to give up tilling the land and hoeing the garden and to live happily in their own homes with their wives. Those who do not have a wife would spend their time lounging in the outhouses and dining at the taravad. It has also been decided that if there are women unfortunate enough not to have husbands, the taravad should grant them a definite sum of money calculated to cover the expenses of clothing, bathing oil, ornamentation and other personal needs. If women obtain any personal property from their husbands, that accrues to the taravad after their deaths.

After their studies are over the men are allowed to enter into sambandham with a suitable woman of a well-disposed family of the same caste, with due respect to their own wishes and the wishes of their parents and elders. They are assigned some lands from the taravad and a dwelling place, and told to take a share of the income enough for their needs, entrusting the rest to the taravad. At any time, a man well liked by most of the members of the taravad functions as general administrator, and the others live by helping and obeying him. This is the system in our taravad.

Now, if I don't say a little bit about the place where I live now, that is, my husband's home, the readers won't be able to make sense when I talk about my everyday routine. But I shan't take too long either. My husband's home is around six *katam*s [the equivalent of ten miles] north of our locality, in Ernad. 'Kottappurattu Kizhakkedattu' is their name. Their family and ours have been related to each other for a long time. Though the two families are somewhat similar in rank, honour, wealth and in mode of management, recently, some members have begun to get slightly crazy over English education and government jobs, and thus there are one or two B.A. holders, who have got into suitable jobs. Some of the younger ones are also getting higher education. Seeing them do this, we too did likewise, sending two young ones from our family to study English. But what happened was that Kuttikrishnan, the son of my elayamma (younger maternal aunt) fell ill soon after passing the B.A. exam, and his younger brother, Sankarankutty, didn't pass the Matriculation, even after four attempts. Therefore, our senior menfolk decided that it wouldn't be safe to wander far beyond our ancestral profession of farming, and the madness didn't grow much worse.

The practice of introducing all children to letters at the age of five, and educating girls till the age of sixteen and boys till they turn twenty has prevailed in our taravad since olden times. A scholarly and sensible *asan* [a teacher] is made to live with us for this purpose, and he is paid well. My father too belonged to the above-mentioned Kizhakkedattu house. His name was Rarappunni Nair, and he was well-liked and well known. But unfortunately, neither myself, my brother Appu nor sister Kalyanikutty could enjoy his affections for very long; it is pointless to regret now. He passed away unexpectedly in the terrible smallpox epidemic, which spread in the northern areas including Ernad and Valluvanad in 1059 [1883–84]. He was thirty-two at that time. Some astrologers have said that his horoscope contained the *dwitramshadyogam*. Well, I have no clue about what that is. It's world-famous that our *valiammaman* [great-granduncle][4] who passed away in 1075 [1899–1900], was a very famous master of astrology, knowing all about past, present and future. His sister, our *muttassi* [great-grandmother] who is still with us, has told us many times that he would always say that he would die only after seeing a thousand full moons, and it happened just like that. He passed away at the age of eighty-four. Until his death, he would stay all prepared whenever there was a birth due in the family. Thus, on hearing the time at which my mother had delivered her third child, he got up from his seat and, not uttering a word to anyone, walked some distance up and down, his hand upon his head and sighing in between. I heard that he then retired to his room, saying: 'Sad indeed! What is fated cannot be stalled. Only the tall and healthy coconut tree will be struck by lightning.' Be that as it may, my father died the day after Kalyanikutty's first birthday. I was five when *acchan* [father] died and Appu, three. My mother was only twenty-seven. But as is the practice in our taravad, she did not take another husband.

The scholar-valiammaman, I mentioned earlier, was far fonder of my father than any other person having a sambandham in our family. He had a special soft spot for him. More so because Mother is the daughter of his own sister's daughter. Because of all this, after the death of our father, he kept me and my brother Appu close to him, and brought us up under his direct supervision. He was also particularly attentive to my mother's needs and well being. My valiammaman was the senior-most member in the taravad. In his youth, he had been very mindful of learning. After being educated locally, he went away at the beginning of his youth without telling anyone, travelling in distant lands for some ten or fifteen years, returning to become a great *advaitin* and an ascetic. Yet, as is often seen among some of these types, he didn't want solitude, didn't cook for himself, didn't practice bizarre ascetic practices or meditation, and didn't wear an ascetic's garments. Common worldly people would not have the kind of skill he had of being amiable to the world. As I mentioned earlier, he usually sat in the upper-storey of the outhouse on the south side of the taravad. Appu and I were his ever-present attendants. We also slept in his room at night. The grand old man would wake unfailingly at dawn, at 4 am. We would also be woken up then. Our faces washed, we would be made to repeat the holy chants. We would also finish brushing our teeth and other ablutions before dawn. The teacher would then come and call us to our lessons. We studied on the lower storey of that very outhouse, lessons going on till about nine. Then valiammaman would call us to bathe and pray. He didn't fancy going out without us. After prayers we would eat beside him, and then climb up to the upper storey of the outhouse. After lunch, the teacher would call us again, and we would go downstairs to study.

Like this, we learnt to read and write quite well by the age of ten or twelve and gained some depth in Sanskrit too. In mid-afternoon, valiammaman himself would teach us a little bit of the *kavyams*, the *natakams*; he would make us read Malayalam works like the *Ramayanam, Bharatam, Bhagavatam, Krishnagatha* and so on, and make us tell the meanings. He would read out sections which we could not manage with elegance and devotion, and explain the meaning to us. Though a great scholar in Sanskrit, he harboured great respect for and interest in Malayalam works. He found the contempt displayed by some self-claimed Sanskrit pundits towards Malayalam works quite insufferable. He thought Ezhuttachan's works to be most enlightening, and *Krishnagatha* to be most entertaining. He would repeat at least ten times a day that 'rooms without light, and minds without the puranas are no good'. He was indeed the man who had seen the unseen sides of the arts of curing children's ailments and making antidotes for poisons. Many have been astounded by his tricks. But for this, everything must be brought to him, under him, as he says.[Without this] even if the call came from the palace of the Maharaja, he would not step out. He had said that an ascetic taught these two subjects to him. Though he tried to show us many of his special skills, it had only the effect of pouring water upon sand. But even the simple things that he taught us stand us in good stead now. I know not how to express my respect for and gratitude to him, now that I know through experience the wisdom of the advice he gave me many times, that nothing is so important for a woman as the knowledge of cures for children's illnesses. Tears prick me, I shiver with feelings; they do not cease to stir me even today, as I recollect the story of my childhood, which passed under the care and guidance of that great soul.

The days of my childhood passed thus, and were nearly over. My fortunes underwent a great change at my eighteenth year. If the full fruition of a woman's life lies in her obtaining a husband worthy of her in birth, form, age, learning, wealth and so on, I have, indeed, reached the pinnacle of good fortune. For women who are unfortunate by birth, what greater fortune can accrue, other than having someone to share with affection and trust in all their thoughts and musings?

Suffice to say that from that day onwards, I attained the status of a homemaker. From then on, except for Onam or any other special occasion, I don't usually come to the home of my birth. I've already described the ways in my husband's taravad somewhat. He is the fifth among men there [fifth oldest man in the taravad]. At that time, he was twenty-seven years old. Though he isn't very handsome—fair and chubby like a poovan banana—he has a very pleasant face, medium complexion and a tall, strong, healthy body. He had been studying for a B.A; but because of some incidental hitches, he couldn't appear for the exam for some years, and then the matter has lain like that ever since. But because of his remarkable intellect and diligence in reading books, ordinary B.A holders daren't say anything to him off-hand. Though he holds the English in high regard for their industriousness, he does have some contempt for the crafty tricks some of them play, and scorns some of our English-crazy young men who fall prey to these tricks and their tomfoolery. For this reason, some such people aren't shy of calling him 'green-eyed' or 'uncivilized'.[5] However, many cultured men well versed in English often visit us to listen to his sound and sober arguments and enjoy his company, and stay on for a day or two. [He argues] 'Is it not our foolishness that we imitate the Englishmen in certain matters in which differences in situations and practices have been wrought by difference in community, religion and nationality? Is there a single one among them who will imitate us in such things? We inhabit a country, which is a very hot part of the world; it is bad for us to always wear hats and shirts like the white people who live in very cold areas. Because white folk have only hats, shirts, socks, etc., and not clothes similar to ours, when they say 'dressing', it refers to donning these garments. Since 'dressing' seems to refer to wearing hats, shirts, etc., and not to our practice, even when we are well-dressed in our own manner, it is as if our clothes were not clothes, and their garments alone would count as such. If this besotted condition which lets them get away with such an interpretation is not idiocy, then what is it?'

'[He says] in a land in which a great number of trees, plants and creepers provide us with leaves, flowers and roots that nourish and strengthen our bodies, why waste money and energy to plant near the house, creepers and plants that do not have any such use? Is it not more profitable and pleasurable to foster creepers like jasmines and flowering plants like tulsi and rose, and plantains, brinjal plants, yams and other plants, and fruit-bearing creepers such as bitter-gourd, snake-gourd, beans, pumpkin, etc., and trees like lemon, mango, pomegranate and so on, instead of these?'

It is questions such as these that earn him the dislike of the sophisticated set. However, we live on one of the agricultural properties owned by his taravad. Our house is a small one with a *nalukettu* with a west-facing upper storey. The front compound is a rather spacious, even ground. It is a decent garden, filled with coconut palms, mango trees, jackfruit trees, plants like plantain and brinjal and seasonal creepers like pumpkin, and is always green and pretty with flowers and fruits of various sorts, with not a bit of land gone waste. Around it there are fields rich in yield and sown three times a year. The area of almost one or one and a half-square miles are under his supervision. He has also the necessary labour and cattle and cows for its maintenance. Except for festive occasions like Onam and Vishu every day is a working day. When I came here, a cook and a sweeper were the sole inhabitants. Once I came, I was given charge of everything, the complete responsibility of domestic tasks, keeping things safe, locking up the valuables and so on. I could see that because he had to go out and concentrate on the farming, he was getting lax about other things. So I had to be particularly alert about these.

Just my luck that in a short while, he began to be very pleased with my doings and ways, and trusted me well! With this, I began to be even more vigilant about my tasks. Some four years passed thus, the tree of our matrimony blossomed for the first time, and we had a little boy, the very essence of our mutual love. When he was about three, merciful God once again caused a pleasing little vine to sprout, as the reflection of our affection for, and trust in each other. The *makam* star in the coming month of *Kumbham* [February–

March] is her fifth birthday. We live bathing all our five senses with ecstasy, at the sight of these two little ones.

Now, I shall stop after describing briefly my daily routine, which my dear friends may not savour much, though it is extremely palatable to me. My routine, which I got used to partly under my valiammaman influence, and which I altered according to my needs after my coming here, is like this: I wake up early at four, at dawn. At once, I ready the necessaries for chewing betel leaves, place it on the betel-plate, and come downstairs. Then I sweep the nalukettu, the eastern part of the house, and the front veranda, and light a lamp towards the entrance of the nalukettu. Soon afterwards, I wash my face and feet, and churn the curds singing my prayers in between. Then, I sweep the house, the front compound, and plaster the verandas with cow-dung paste. After the curds are churned, I go to the kitchen, put out last night's pots and pans to be washed, sweep and plaster the floor. I wash one small pot by myself, and make some gruel in it with pounded rice. By then, it will be nearly six-thirty. By the time the gruel is done, he will be up and outside, gone off to send the labourers to their work. He will then come into the nalukettu after his morning ablutions. There wouldn't be too many side dishes to go with the gruel. I fry and store for five or six days whatever tasty tubers we have around the season: plantains, jackfruit, yams. That would usually do. And then, maybe, two toasted pappadams and tender mango pickle. He couldn't do without freshly churned buttermilk. When he eats, he must have Kuttikrishnan and Kalyanikutty on his two sides—otherwise he would not be at ease. By the time he finishes the gruel and washes his hands, I will be upstairs, readying the betel leaves—I would keep one in the hand, to be chewed then and the rest to be taken to the fields, I put in the *madichellam* [box, tied around the waist]. After chewing betel-leaves, he takes his *olakkuda* [cadjan-leaf umbrella], puts on his slippers and goes out. On stepping out of the nalukettu, he never fails to throw back a quick glance. I don't have to tell you that I've to stand in the nalukettu, ready, so that the glance could be aimed only at my face.

By now, it would be almost seven or seven-thirty. Then my job is to chop everything necessary for lunch. The side dishes are all prepared from whatever grows in our garden. Usually, there would be one sour side dish, and two non-sour ones. There must be sambar and mulakushyam, or kalan, olan, mezhukupuratti [all typically Malayali dishes that go with rice]. Chukkuvellam [spiced warm water] is always served. I would have to keep a special eye on these two. Then, a measure of good, ripened rice, washed well, without stones and grains of paddy, cooked not too soft, not too hard—just right—and that would be perfect! We also couldn't do without pickles, freshly churned buttermilk and cleaned salt. That is the spread for lunch.

Once all the items for cooking lunch are ready, I would go and take a bath and start to milk the cows. We always have four or five cows to milk. Sometimes, there would be buffaloes to milk also. But that's just too much to handle and so the servant does it. By then it would be nearly eleven o'clock. He would have returned from the fields by then. I would be present on the veranda, ready with a mug of water to wash his feet, and betel-leaves for him to chew. He would rest a bit after washing his feet, chewing the betel-leaves, and brushing his teeth, and in between, he would tell me all about the servants that day, how many men, women and children were out that day, and how they were working. When he was done with brushing his teeth, he would go for his bath, and in that time, I would have measured out the *valli* [wages in kind] for the labourers, and left it in separate heaps on the floor of the front room. He didn't take much time to bathe. When he returned, Kuttikrishnan and Kalyanikutty would be ready with fresh clothes, *bhasmam* [sacred ashes], sandal paste and a mirror, and they would be hurrying him, drooling over the prospect of lunch!

In the meanwhile I would have set out the plantain leaves [these were used as serving plates, and are still used in ceremonial feasts] and the wooden seats in the nalukettu.

The leaves should never be less than three! Though we have a cook to serve the dishes, he and the children aren't comfortable if they don't get some titbits from my hands. That's because, they claim, if the side dishes aren't very tasty, it wouldn't feel so bad if I served them! Ripe plantains are usually plentiful because we grow so many of them. However, he doesn't like to have them regularly for lunch. But on some summer days when I could see that he was worn out a bit more from the sun, I would place two well-ripened, peeled *padatti* [Ernadan plantains] upon his leaf just as he is about to finish lunch. There is a look that he would give me then, all mixed with a smile. As that is such a limitless reward to all my labours, I never miss a single chance to reap that profit.

After lunch, he usually walks for about half an hour inside the nalukettu, repeating holy chants. I eat my lunch in that interval. Then we would go up to the *talam* [a room that is open on one side at least] upstairs, chew betel-leaves, and rest awhile, lying down and enjoying Kuttikrishnan's and Kalyanikutty's jokes. Then it would be nearly two. The children would go off to the school, as they did in the mornings. He too would set off for the fields with umbrella, betel-leaves and slippers I would go with him some distance, and then come back to sit in the talam to read the Puranas for a while, not letting slip what valiyammaman had inculcated in me. The *Ramayanam* and the *Bhagavatam*, I would read every day. On the days he did not have to go to the fields, he would join me. Some days, he would be lost in devotion; that day the *Bhagavatam* would be read. Sometimes it would be all reasoning, and that day the topic would most definitely be the *Ramayanam*. And if erudition took precedence on some days, those days would be marked for the *Bharatam* or the *Krishnagatha*. But I would brush the dust off the great ornaments bestowed to me by valiammaman every day. He has gained some understanding of the words through frequent reading, and being by nature very intelligent and endowed with taste, is able to grasp the essence of poetry quite well.

After reading, preparations for dinner begin. I chop what is needed to be cooked for dinner, wipe and tidy up things in the bedroom, clean all that neded cleaning, sweep and swab the floor, lay out the beds properly and open all the windows, and go downstairs to see whether the nalukettu, the veranda and other rooms have been properly swept. Then I ready the lamp to be lit in the evening, filling it with oil and making the wicks. Afterwards, the cows that are to be milked in the evening are milked. I see whether the grass for the cows and the calves has been readied, and get them tied properly after giving them gruel and oil cakes. Then it would be around five-thirty. Again, as in the morning, I measure out the labourers' wages and light the lamp after having a wash. He would have returned from work by then. Except for *Ekadashi* and the new moon, he has an oil bath every day. Let me mention in between that during *Ekadashi*, he never fails to fast the whole day, keep awake at night, and read the *Bhagavatam*. I go to wash myself only after getting together everything for the oil-bath in the bath house. He insists on hot water for the oil-bath. Coming back from the fields, he washes his feet, changes his waistcloth, chews betel-leaves and walks for some time in the garden, asking the children about their lessons and teaching them a bit, until the sweat dries. He then bathes, and spends some time reciting the sacred chants. The time would be around eight o'clock. Then he has dinner, and walks for sometime afterwards, as he does in the afternoon. I would have my dinner in between. Then we go upstairs and spend our time in some literary amusement, and go to bed by ten o'clock. I never sleep without him sleeping first.

This is what my homemaking is like.

From 'Ente Jeevacharitravum Grihinidharmavum', *Lakshmibhayi*, 2, 12, M.E. 1082 Meenam (Mar-Apr 1907): 529–47.

Notes

1. The *Report of the Malabar Marumakkathayam Commission*, however, did remark on the lingering of polyandry among the Nairs of the very same area, in the Ponnani and Valluvanad taluks of Malabar. See *Report* (Madras 1891: 83). The author seems very keen to indicate here, and later, that her family does not practice polyandry or widow-remarriage. Such practices, it may be remembered were frowned upon by Nair reformism, which was generally committed to 'sexual discipline'.
2. *Sambandham* refers to the sanctioned sexual relations among the matrilineal castes, which lingered on in Kerala well into the mid-twentieth century. In sambandham (lit. 'relationship'), the woman was not transferred to the husband's property/kin group, and the children of the union belonged to the mother's family, even when women did live with their husbands along with the children of the union. The woman often never left her natal home, nor did the husband gain full sexual or material rights over her. As implied here, *sambandham* often implied hypergamy.
3. In fact, the very granting of these tenancies would be the indirect affirmation of one's status as *janmi* (landlord).
4. In matrilineal families one's mother's/grandmother's brother, usually older brother, occupied the senior most position, and was indeed had more control over one that either the father/grandfather.
5. This and the following argument are probably samples provided by the author of the husband's sharp thinking. That is why she has used quotation marks around 'green-eyed' and 'uncivilized'.

4
K. P. M.

The author is not known. There are, however, some indications that the author is upper caste and from the northern parts of Kerala.

Are Women Weak?

The appellation *abala* is commonly applied to women. The dictionary also claims that *Stree yoshid abala yosha* [the various synonyms of 'woman' in the Sanskrit lexicon, the *Amarakosa*]. However, is this link a coincidental one, as in *dhittham* [elephant] or is it literal, as in the case of words like *pankajam* [lotus, literally 'born of the mud']? If we take the latter to be true then *abala* would surely mean 'she who lacks strength'. Then the question naturally arises about the comparison: lacking in strength compared to whom? It is generally accepted that the comparison is with Man.

When we talk of strength, the primary reference is mainly to physical robustness. Some would consider the vitality of intelligence. Even when both these are acknowledged, our history and present experience reveal that women are not lacking in strength compared to men. One essential aspect needs to be considered here first. Is strength (irrespective of whether this refers to the body or the mind) given at birth? Or, is it an accomplishment? If the comparison is to be made of inborn strength, the mental and physical abilities of a boy and a girl must be tested and compared at their maturity, after bringing them up in exactly the same way after birth, with equal amount and kind of nutrition, without allowing physical or mental activity. If it is the acquired strength that is referred to, then the two children must be brought up mostly in this way, but with the same sort of education, in the same periods, and then their relative mental skills must be ascertained and compared.

Even if we must attribute some significance to the fact that women do undergo some important experiences like menstruation and pregnancy unlike men in their early youth, if obstacles like child marriage honoured by some jatis among the Hindus are removed, then it may well be claimed that almost up to the age of twenty, women are as capable of education as men. If that education is uninterrupted and assiduously undertaken, women may obtain a fair degree of erudition and mental development. It is entirely inappropriate, and indeed a shame, that nothing of this sort is undertaken. Women are given off to undeserving men at the age of ten or twelve as bonded slaves, and their mental and physical powers are left uncultivated, through binding them to cooking jobs and other domestic chores that are easily done.

Now, it may be proved that women are not weaker than men by our present experience, without resorting to the experiments just suggested. Let us first consider the aspect of physical strength. Compare the daily routines of a common householder and a common housewife. The wife is already up many hours before the man, and has embarked upon her self-mortification amidst fire on all four sides, and the sun above (*panchagni*),[1] after finishing off the sweeping, plastering of floors with dung-paste and the washing of dishes. She is relieved of this at least partially for some rest, only well after breakfast, close to the afternoon. Even that hour is filled with many chores to be done. If the woman has a couple of children besides, one of them at her breast, one need hardly describe her travails. Preparations for the evening's fare will commence around two o'clock. Once begun, this struggle with fire and water, quite like the drudgery of coolies in a steam engine, will go on till past eight o'clock at night. Who performs such labour, which has to be carried on constantly, with no respite, come rain or shine, three hundred and sixty-five days a year, and no holidays, but the abalas?

Let us now think of the labourers and the farmers. Among them, men do the work of tilling the field with bullocks, hoeing, chopping wood, climbing coconut palms, and so on. Women, however, carry ashes, cow dung and hides upon their heads, and mix it in the soil as manure, stand knee-deep in muddy and watery fields to pluck and plant the saplings, do the weeding, harvest the grain and carry the stacks, thresh, winnow, fan and clean the paddy, cut the grass and gather the straw to feed the cattle, pound the paddy, distil toddy and palm sugar, pound coconut husk, decay it and twist the fibre into coir, weave the coconut leaves for thatches, weave many sorts of mats and cloth, cut and dry coconut kernels and extract the oil, besides engaging in may other sorts of labour and crafts. Careful reflection will make it obvious that it is the womenfolk who pursue most of our crafts. Moreover, among the jatis lower down in the Shudra category, such as the Mappila, Tiyya, Kanakka, Cheruma, Paraya, Nayadi, and so on, women do most of the mentally and physically demanding work, and over longer hours. I do believe that all impartial and alert observers will agree with me on this point.

The arduous labour performed by the Brahmin women among the upper castes, will astound the other castes, and indeed, put them to shame. Among the *Paradesi* (i.e. mostly Tamil) Brahmins, a clerk or teacher earning a pittance of ten or twelve rupees, will live in comfort anywhere, be it Cochin [Kochi], Calicut [Kozhikode] or Quilon [Kollam], with his wife and children, he minding his work, and his wife, all the domestic work and the care of children. They need no manservant, no maid. Look at the situation in the homesteads of the Nambutiris [the Malayala Brahmins], who are esteemed for their wealth and noble birth. In many of these homes, which require one or two *paras*[2] of rice and adequate quantities of side dishes to go along with for a meal, the entire burden of the cooking is borne by two or three Antharjanams [Malayala Brahmin women] all by themselves. What is more, even during feasting on occasions like the Othoottu,[3] these women gather some of their female relatives to prepare all the dishes quite effortlessly. Even Valalan[4] himself would bow in assent if he saw these moon-faced maidens lift up huge brass vessels brimming with hot cooked rice with their bangle-adorned, vine-like, delicate arms and coolly tilt them to drain off the rice-gruel, in full view of their heartless men. Simply compare the fare prepared by the Mukkani Pattanmar of the *agrasala* at Thiruvananthapuram,[5] or the dishes cooked in the *valiya adukkala* of the Vaikom temple, where the Muttassu Nambutiri and his assistants,[6] sweaty, smoke-smothered, teary-eyed and forever blowing their noses, toil on dishes, eight out of ten of which are unfit to be placed upon the tongue, with those cooked with nonchalant ease by these jewels of Womanliness; the comparison itself will be rendered superfluous. Though there are very many such instances to cite further, I leave them to the readers who may think of them by themselves.

Let us now think of mental strength. She was in the midst of all possible worldly comforts, along with her husband, the very Perfection of Virtue, who had broken the bow of Sriparameswara to win her hand. He was to be crowned heir of the kingdom, and preparations were on for the event. Then, suddenly, he was summoned to his father's presence, and on returning, he announced the following to her:[7]

> 'Know this, my father has given to me
> The kingdom of the Dandaka forest
> Wherein is to lie my deeds of merit.
> Beloved, live on without sorrow.
> There will I pass, full fourteen years

> *To return, the harm dispersed.*
> *Dissuade me not; cast no doubt*
> *In my path; forsake your grief.*
> *Abide well, my mother by your side.'*

To a husband who took his leave so casually, so unexpectedly, she replied thus, without the slightest twitch of emotion:

> *'I will march ahead to the forest,*
> *Noble One, you need only follow.*
> *Know this, Noble Heart, our parting*
> *Can never ever be worthy.'*

Is not the tenacity of mind shown by that radiant-faced woman who replied thus, truly matchless? On hearing her, the husband began:

> *'How do I take you to forests dense*
> *Where beasts swarm, wild and strong,*
> *Rakshasas who dine on human flesh?*
> *The very sight strikes terror in all.*
> *In women, 'tis said, fear abides most.*
> *Sweet lass, the roots, the fruits*
> *Sour potions, will be your food.*
> *No tasty food, drink so pure,*
> *No sweet milk, in all the days.*
> *The paths are rough; they go*
> *High and low, darkly tunnelled,*
> *Strewn with thorns.*
> *We know not our way, and*
> *May not seek it through, for*
> *No one treads in forests deep.*
> *The biting cold, the aching bones,*
> *Journeying on by foot alone,*
> *Face-to face with Rakshasas.*
> *Terrible this, you must know*
> *Hard to live and hard to bear.'*

Thus did he try to deter her, describing the horrors and unendurable trials of life in the jungles. However, she responded, unswayed:

> 'Can any other cause harm to me
> When I dwell constantly by your side?
> The roots, the fruits, the water,
> What you leave upon your plate
> Make for me ambrosia, Divine Nectar.
> Thorns so sharp, stones so jagged
> Turn petal-soft beneath my feet
> When I walk with my husband.
> Leave me not; I have no fear
> Nor will I cause you any grief,
> Husband of mine, tender lover.'

Does not Sita's unwavering mind astonish even great men? (Likewise, remember the great hardiness of mind exhibited by Panchali, the wife of the Pandavas, Damayanti, the beloved consort of King Nala, and Savitri herself. Why go that far; since we have explicit examples in Empress Victoria, who has protected us like a mother for more than sixty years, Rani Setu Parvati Bai of Travancore (Tiruvitamkoor) and many others, additional instances are quite unnecessary.

From 'Streekal Abalakalano', *Lakshmibhayi*, 3, 8, M.E. 1083 Vrischikam (Nov–Dec 1907–08): 329–36.

Notes

1 In the myths, great austerities are performed in the midst of the *panchagni*, fire on all four sides and above.
2 A large local measure of weight, equal to ten *idangazhi*s; one *para* of grain weighs approximately six kg.
3 Refers to traditional recitation of the Yajurveda by the Nambutiris, which lasts a whole month. During each day of the *othoottu*, feasts were prepared.

4   A male cook. In the *Mahabharatam*, during their exile, in the period where they had to live incognito, this was the name taken by the Pandava Bhima who disguised himself as a cook at the court of Virata.

5   In the large kitchens at the Padmanabha Swamy temple at Thiruvananthapuram where large numbers of Brahmins were fed every day, the food being prepared by the Mukkani Pattanmar, a certain class of Tamil Brahmins who wore their hair with the forelock.

6   Literally, the 'big kitchen' at the Shiva temple at Vaikom, where the famous *Praṭal Sadya* (breakfast), a major offering, is prepared. The chief cook at Vaikom temple is traditionally a Nambutiri from the Muttassu family, and he is assisted by Nairs from sixteen families (the *Patinaranmar*).

7   From Tunchattu Ramanujan Ezhuttachan's *Adhyaytma Ramayanam*.

5

K. CHINNAMMA

K. Chinnamma (1882–1930) was born in Attingal near Thiruvananthapuram in a Nair family. She studied at the Zenana Mission Girls' School and the Maharajah's College for Women, Thiruvananthapuram. She passed the F.A. (First Arts) examination (held at the end of the first year of college) in 1908 and joined the Education Department of Tiruvitamkoor as Assistant Inspectress. Her involvement in Nair reformism began at the Nair Conference at Perunna in 1911, and her speech there, which was highly critical of the reformers' inattention to assigning women a positive role in reformism, attracted considerable attention. She moved to Kollam in 1912, and was very active in organizing women's associations there. In 1918, she began the Shree Mulam Shashtyabhdapoorthy Smaraka Hindu Mahila Mandiram at Thiruvananthapuram, an institution for educating and training poorer girls. She resigned her job, and became a full-time worker for the Mandiram. The activities of the Mandiram were much lauded in the 1920s; it even published a women's magazine called the Mahila Mandiram. It still functions in Poojapura, Thiruvananthapuram. Her biographer mentions that the article below was actually a speech made by her (Balakrishnan Nair 1947: 66–68).

The Place of Women in Education

Genuine education surely aims at the refinement of the mind and the development of the intellect. Therefore, a human being remains a student all his life. This does not, however, mean that the entire period must be actually spent in a school. The whole of worldly existence truly constitutes a school. Our study must be completed first in our homes, then in schools, and later by our own labour. If our life's mission is to be attained, then the persons responsible for our development in each of these stages of life must aptly carry out the tasks necessary at each stage. The lessons we learn at home hold an extraordinary sway over us, compared to other influences, and the instruction gained from other institutions relies heavily on these early lessons. Ordinary people take heed of training that is received at school alone. This is a gross mistake. There can be little doubt that seeking to acquire other sorts of instruction without creating a strong base of first providing training at home is akin to building forts or houses without laying proper foundations. A just-born infant is completely innocent, lacking in any sense of discretion. However, since the human being is prone to imitation by nature, the child begins to copy the behaviour of those who are most intimate with it. The persons who enter such affectionate contact with the infant are surely its parents. Of the two parents, the mother is closer. In our early infancy, we are cared for and protected by our mothers. Because fathers have many other obligations to fulfil, we are not subjected to his loving attentions to such a great extent. Therefore, as infants, we tend to emulate carefully all the gestures of our mother, who is dearest to our hearts. Thus, all the mother's words, actions and advice fall directly upon the mirror of the mind.

'The young mind and white paper are alike, whatever is written on both leaves its mark.' However, we can destroy a piece of paper with bad writing. That which gets stamped on the mind cannot be destroyed thus. It remains inscribed on one's mind until one's death. Therefore it is clear that all the words and ideals that we imbibe from our parents, without even being conscious of this process, occupy a permanent place in our minds, and that the home is the first school. Parents, and all those who cherish the community, must become alert to the necessity of maintaining the home as an ideal centre of learning.

The modern pedagogic precept that 'one example is worth a thousand sermons' is indeed a sound one. We must constantly remember that maxims like 'Woman Is the Creator of a Jati', or that 'One Good Mother Has the Influence of a Thousand Teachers' are not exaggerations. We assimilate the virtues that ensure happiness in our lives, and enable us to realize the mission of our existence, from our mothers. These would be—faith in God, obedience, truth, compassion, non-violence, humility, moral consciousness, simplicity—the mother must foster all these in our minds. Parents must constantly remember that a boy can be raised according to our wishes only by giving him the right training. The responsibility of correcting deficiencies in children's character, and directing them towards the path of virtue lies with the parents.

'The habits of childhood, will they be forgotten, ever!' Common, everyday happenings may be enough to convince us that this insight is not foolishness. It is thus clear that the mental growth, intellectual refinement, acquisition of good habits and character, and so on, must take place at home, and the major share of the responsibility for this rests with the mother.

Besides, a homemaker should properly discharge her duty in the important obligation of taking care of children. The food and clothing of children must be chosen and balanced well to ensure their good health. The food that they are given must be of the sort that improves their mental faculties; it must not dull them. Hygiene is very necessary in children's clothing. In these two matters, our mothers are found to be unforgivably negligent. They are concerned with merely filling up the child's belly and little more—they have no thought of what detrimental effects the food may have and how these may be alleviated.

I have seen in my experience many mothers grind the food meant for adults, and feed it to children, out of sheer laziness to prepare separate food for children. Children thus ingest food substances that may impair their digestion. Even when corrected, mothers remain unconcerned. There are also many that are hesitant to spend on special food for children. Yet, the reluctance to bear this negligible loss will cause lifelong regret. Without proper food, children turn sickly by the age of four or five and they are packed off to school. Children who are nurtured in this faulty fashion lack the ability to absorb what is taught in class, and so we will not get the desired results from them. Therefore before children are sent to learn in the school, mothers should fulfil their obligations properly, and see to it that their children have attained as much physical and mental strength as possible, and are capable of performing their school tasks.

The mother's duty in the years before the child goes to school is clear now. Now let us consider whether the mother and other family members have any responsibility in instructing the children after they have been entrusted to teachers. Before the seed in sown in a field, it has to be tilled well, and enough manure must be applied. All the weeds that may hamper seed growth must be removed time to time. Only then will we harvest ripe and full fruit. In education too, this is the method to be followed. Preparing children's minds and bodies for schooling so that they will appreciate the knowledge given in the school and produce good results this is the task of none other than the mother. For this, the mother must pay attention to the food, play, sleep, arrangements for study, and the conduct of children.

Regarding food, just as they neglect paying attention to what children need to eat in infancy, mothers are quite neglectful of what children who are going to school need to eat. The whole of Man's well-being, spiritual and material, depend heavily upon his health. Health itself is heavily dependent upon food, bathing, and so on. Ordinary people are bothered only to pack some sort of food as lunch and send children to school; they do not care about its good and bad effects. The Bhagavad Gita tells us how food substances may be divided into *satvik*, *rajas* and *tamas* types. Satvik foods assure longevity, strength, enthusiasm, good health, comfort and pleasure; foods that are bitter, sour or hot, the *rajas* foods, bring sorrow and disease; and the *tamas* foods, which are stale, tasteless, smelly and the leftovers of a meal, aggravate the dark side of human nature. This is what the Lord advises.

That clean food increases the virtuous quality of a person and boosts his perceptive powers is testified by the *Shrutis*. From this it is evident that the mother should pick and choose for children those foods that improve their perceptive powers and steady their minds and that all of us need to give special importance to the matter of food. Only then will the child be able to study well in school. Among us, children who stay the whole day without eating are not at all rare. There are two important reasons why this happens. First, the poverty of the parents. While we cannot blame anyone harshly for this sorry situation, it may be said that once the parents have resolved to educate their children, they must step up efforts to improve their condition through sufficient labour, keeping in mind the intention with which children are sent to school.

Secondly, let us consider the distance between the school and the home. If the school is too far away from the home, the mother must ensure that the child has lunch at school, without coming all the way home. Thirdly, fear of violating established customs or superstitions. Unfortunately, it is the Nairs, who are mostly prey to this. In some places children leave for school early in the morning, and are allowed to eat only after they return, after a bath. The fear of the parents [mothers] that contact with children of other castes and creeds will be polluting, forces children to fast thus. These mothers do not realize that their superstition makes their children vulnerable to illness, destroys their power of comprehension, finally to make them useless, out of the sheer lack of food.

In the same way, there is plenty of negligence in the matter of clothing as well. If any teacher insists on clean clothes in school, he is denounced. There are but a few who would reflect on why he insisted so, and on the disadvantages of rejecting his advice. Clean clothes, like clean food, enhance the child's health. Bathing children every day too builds their health and the intelligence, and hence must not be neglected. It is because of the utter laxity of the mothers that we see most children in ordinary schools suffering from scabies and eczema. This is also becoming a distinct impediment to the progress of learning.

The next subject that deserves the mother's attention is the utilization of the time which children spend at home after school hours. It was mentioned earlier that contrary to popular perception, learning is not contingent upon schooling alone. Teachers and parents have to work in unison if education has to be fruitful. Children are generally fearful of teachers. Their actual thoughts are hardly revealed at school. Their real nature surfaces at home, and at play. It is the duty of the parents to closely probe their behaviour in these situations and weed out promptly any undesirable traits. Since discretion is weak in children, they may be tempted to indulge in minor vices like stealing books, pencils and other objects belonging to their classmates. It is the mother's duty to scrutinize all this, and award appropriate correction or punishment. Mothers, who encourage such corruption instead of nipping them in the bud, are also not unknown. Even when badness is not explicitly encouraged, the tendency to foist all the burdens of correction upon the teacher opens the path to many dangers. The child who steals a pencil may grow into a seasoned criminal, only to end up in prison. Mother and son will then repent in vain. Motherly Duty entails that adequate precaution is taken to assure that such a situation never materialises.

Again, the sensible mother should inquire about the child's conduct, study and position at school. Arrangements must be made for study at home too. A mother has so much responsibility as far as the education of a child is concerned.

A teacher is in charge of very many children in his class, and is bound to impart a certain portion of knowledge to the pupils within a fixed time-period. He may not be able to satisfy all children always. Since the capacity to assimilate knowledge varies between children, the teacher cannot be blamed too much. Fear may prevent children from standing up in class and clearing their doubts. In such instances, children will usually come home, and try to allay their doubts at their beloved mother's side. Undertaking to clear such doubts at home, and checking the homework is the duty of mothers, and it will ease the workload of both children and teachers.

Next, mothers should diligently instil the faith in God in children. A school can impart only materialistic instruction. Therefore, we need to make other provisions for our spiritual enlightenment. This should begin at home. This great virtue holds the key to our well-being. Only through it will superior qualities like horror of evil and humility take root. Hence this too counts among the duties of mothers; they must provide their offspring with a satisfactory guide through life so that they do not lose their way and produce good results.

If each mother would set her heart upon the adequate fulfilment of the the duties just mentioned, every child would be able to reap the full benefits of education. A misconception rampant among us is that the primary purpose of education is salaried employment and the creation of wealth through it. We may well guess where the life of a successful gentleman armed with university degrees and wealth would be if he were bereft of such qualities as faith in God, compassion, humility, selflessness, moral consciousness and so on. True education leads us into this many-splendoured good fortune; that we only act in full awareness of the true meaning and purpose of our education. I have offered detailed proof earlier that we are instructed throughout our infancy, childhood and youth, and that the crucial agency in this process lies not with the schoolteacher but with our mothers. Only such mothers deserve to be called so. The major reason why our communities do not attain advancement at the pace we desire lies precisely in the rarity of such enlightened mothers. Hence, the task of those who are dedicated to the community is most certainly the enlightenment of women near and dear to them in homes, through determined efforts to create suitable facilities for their education. Through education, the consciousness that they are the guardians of their children and society in general, that society is itself reliant upon their advancement, may be ignited in the minds of women. This is indispensable for the achievement of both individual and social goals. God blesses those societies in which women are honoured. I need not reiterate that women are the source of both the dignity and indignity of a home or community. If the menfolk turn corrupt and shallow, the repercussions may not be unbearable. However, this discussion has exposed the pernicious effects that ensue from the corruption and shallowness of women.

Women whose minds are cultured with interaction with the virtuous, who lead moral lives, and who are conscious of their duty, ought to be present in every community. May God bless us so that every community is adorned with such women capable of bringing peace and happiness to worldly existence, and raise worthy heirs, great men and women.

From 'Vidyabhyasattil Streekalute Sthanam', *Lakshmibhayi*, 8, 6, M.E. 1088 Kanni (Sept–Oct 1912): 206–18.

6

C. P. Kalyani Amma

Several articles signed similarly appear in the Lakshmibhay, *the journal in which this essay was published, in the early decades of the twentieth century. However, biographical details of this author are not available.*

The Craze for Imitation

I read the article titled 'The Craze for Imitation' by Puttezhattu Raman Menon, B.A.[1] We have been braving the reprimands of ammavamar [uncles][2] and the contempt and derision of people and the newspapers. I am not at all surprised that Mr. Menon has launched a belligerent offensive. Fifteen years back, we were ignorant women, uncultured and half-clad.[3] With much exertion, we secured the permission of mothers and grandmothers to wear the bodice and the jacket. Yet, now that we have managed to cover our bodies appropriately, it seems that all of us have fallen into prodigality! What are we to do now? No matter what the *Keralamahatmyam*[4] or any other sacred text says about the women of Kerala being brought from heaven by Parashurama to satisfy the needs of the *Bhudevas* [Brahmins] about their being exempt from the rules of chastity; about the injunction forbidding them to cover their bodies, there are very few women today who gulp down all this unthinkingly. It is possible that Mr. Menon will agree to the fact that Malayali women have few rivals as far as self-control and modesty are concerned. In most Malayali families, women wake up early, and do not usually eat without bathing, praying and reading the *Ramayanam* or the *Mahabharatam*. If there are among us some who do not go to the temple, pray or read the *Ramayanam* or the *Bharatam* then that is the fault of men. There are many men who roam around with cropped hair,[5] puffing at the cigar or beedi, caring naught for anything, and sporting supercilious postures, ridiculing everyone else simply because they have happened to have passed school, or because their brothers or ammavans have learnt English? The women drinking soda and lemonade at railway stations, and so on, spotted by Mr. Menon were probably fated to be the wives of such men. Why are we, poor weak females, being blamed for this? If women are entrusted to such men who demand that their wives must be handed over to them, secured with a rope, to be 'properly' led, then Mr. Menon may find little consolation. Indeed, he cannot remain reassured that these women will not accept the round-basket and the cock's feather as ornamental headgear.[6]

The next complaint is that we are wasting a great deal of money in our craze for clothes and ornaments. In my family, our debts were cleared off recently by selling off a heavy *poottali* [a necklace in the traditional style] that belonged to my mutassi [grandmother or great grandmother]. Though Mr. Menon may be pleased to see us walk around in that heavy poottali and huge *todas* [large circular ear studs] sticking out on the sides like fancy peacock-feather fans [*alavattom*] we are rather scared that others may ridicule us, or hurl abuse. With a poottali like this, all the ornaments we need, for me, my sisters and the children can be made; some money may even be saved. Yet, it so seems, we are all spendthrifts still! When was more money spent on feasts at ceremonies and rituals, now or then? In the olden days, the *tali* tying ceremony[7] and feast had to be celebrated splendidly, even if all our assets had to be sold. Today many of us feel that such a ceremony is in itself unnecessary. Besides, many mothers conduct the tali-tying in temples along with the infant's rice-giving ceremony.[8] But whatever happens, there seems to be no end to the rebuke that we are squanderers of money.

Mr. Menon seems to be quite disturbed that everyone has forgotten simple songs and melodies like *Odum Mrigangale* and *Kalyani Kalavani*.[9] Yes, many of us have begun to sing the compositions of Thyagaraja and Dikshitar. Mr. Menon is perhaps uncomfortable with this. Though many have given up games and amusements special to Onam and Tiruvatira, none of us has developed fascination for white folk; none of us has begun to imitate their dancing. And that seems quite unlikely a prospect. Though it was Parangoti who said that the vigorous dancing of mostly unclad young women was quite like the Negroes' dance,[10] it must be admitted that there is a grain of truth there. At this rate, Mr. Menon must be rather alarmed that we have lost passion for Mohiniyattam[11] and so on. In older times, holding a Mohiniyattam performance in houses was considered a matter of great prestige. Many enjoyed such entertainment. Since he has found few words to commend the present-day abhorrence of people towards Mohiniyattam, it may be assumed that Mr. Menon would count its decline among the evils of reform.

Mr. Menon is of the opinion that all our ills stem from English education. If all English books were burnt, if all *ravukkas* [blouses] and jackets were dumped in the canal, if the older ornaments found favour with us again and *Kalyani Kalavani* served once more as our major pastime, Mr. Menon's anger towards us may subside a bit. We would like to know what education was that which prompted an Antharjanam—a woman forbidden the very sight of a [*male*] stranger—to take sixty-five paramours and cause them to be cast out of society.[12] Some of us have attained higher education. Some of us occupy prestigious posts. Is it not far more honorable to live a life engaged in some respectable employment rather than to idle it away in depravity? Western women, Tamil women or Parsi women (most of us have not even seen the last-mentioned group) do not dazzle us. Some changes in dressing have been adopted in accordance with changing times. It does not seem necessary to take too seriously the words of those who believe that only such clothes as worn by Adam and Eve are acceptable. Why Mr. Menon should be so deeply perturbed by some women writing their names as 'C. K. Amma' and so on remains quite mysterious. These women do not stick these names on their foreheads. They are not agitated if others call them by their actual names. There is no reason to be alarmed if they use such fancy names in their personal letters, and so on.

On the whole, Mr. Menon's article reminds one of the thrashing meted out by some old karunavanmar [granduncles].[13] They thrash others for good reasons, and for bad reasons. Very often the whipping would be for 'telling the truth', as if that were an offence. There will be very little good to be obtained from them otherwise. How much will others value the whipping or scolding of such karanavanmar? We have received no valuable advice from Mr. Menon. We see that we have been severely upbraided. We do have many faults. If they were recounted in a positive way, no one would have reason to complain. But it will of course be no surprise that we ascribe no value at all to Mr. Menon's article, which has been written with the sole purpose of nagging us.

From 'Anukaranabhramam', *Lakshmibhayi* 10, 12, M.E. 1090 Meenam (March–April 1914–15): 457–63.

Notes

1 Puttezhattu Raman Menon (1889–1973) was a prominent intellectual and public figure in early twentieth-century Kochi (formerly known as Cochin), the government advocate of Kochi, and a District Judge in 1942. He was awarded several literary titles by the Maharaja of Kochi and was also the president of the Kerala Sahitya Akademi. In this article,

Menon launched a vitriolic attack on modern-minded young women as the chief perpetrators of a shallow and superficial modernity. He perceived the major resources of this modernity to derived from blind imitation of Western dress, habits, manners, language, attitudes and tastes. Women, he said were becoming less spiritual and less devoted to their 'God-given' vocation of domestic management. A more balanced 'Response' to the criticism by Kalyani Amma came from him in the next issue, 'Pratyuttaram', *Lakshmibhayi* 11, 1, M.E 1090, Medam (March–April 1914-15): 32–37.

2 Male elders in matrilineal joint families, usually maternal uncles.

3 Refers to earlier female dressing styles in which the bosom was left uncovered, and covering it was considered the mark of the 'loose woman'. See Rajeevan 1999; Devika 1999. For the significance of dress codes in the formation of the modern subject, see Udaya Kumar 1997.

4 *Keralamahatmyam*, which is the Sanskritized version of the *Keralolpatti*, refers to the myth that relates the origin of Kerala to the story of Parashurama. According to this myth, which has many versions (often with significant differences), the landmass of Kerala was reclaimed by Parashurama who gifted it to the Brahmins as expiation for his sin of having massacred the Kshatriyas. Shudra women of Kerala are said to be the descendents of the heavenly damsels brought by him to serve the Brahmins.

5 Change in hairstyle was an important element in breaking away from traditional dress codes in Malayali society; for instance, cutting the tuft (the *kutuma*) was a way of expressing a movement away from the established jati-based social order(s), as evident in several autobiographies remembering early twentieth-century Malayali society. See for instance, Pisharoty 1984.

6 A reference, of course, to the headgear of English women.

7 The *Talikettukalyanam* was a pre-puberty ritual for girls, an expensive affair, especially among the Nairs as well as jatis farther away from the loci of authority, such as the Ezhavas. It was a four-day affair, involving great expense, and hence attacked by reformers. See, for example, Velayudhan 1999. There is now considerable ethnographic literature on the ceremony. For a preliminary survey, see Subramoniam 1993: 692-701.

8 For a brief account of the first feeding ceremony of infants, see Singh 2002: 1119.

9 These were popular songs usually sung in accompaniment to the all-woman dancing during festive or auspicious times (marriages, for instance, among groups higher up in the jati hierarchy) occasions as Onam and Tiruvatira, called Kaikottikkali, or Tiruvatirakali.

10 The reference is to a character in an early text by Kizhakkepattu Ramankutty Menon, called *Parangotiparinayam* (1892) ridiculing the craze for novel writing in Malabar after the success of O. Chandu Menon's *Indulekha* (1889). See Irumbayam 1985. Parangoti is the name of the 'heroine' of this text, who has received modern education that makes her see nothing but error and shame in local ways of life, and ape the racism and ethnocentrism of her white teachers. Here, of course, this sort of racism and ethnocentric posturing works to define Kalyani Amma's reformism itself. This was fundamental to reformism, so much so that even in *Parangotiparinayam*, the dance of the blacks still remains condemned!

11 Mohiniyattam had to await redemption at the hands of the famous Malayali poet Vallattol Narayana Menon later in the century. As is evident here, it was derided as lewd and promiscuous, until Vallattol's efforts at his institution for the performing arts, *Kerala Kala Mandalam*, rescued it from obloquy after a thorough 'sanitizing' operation.

12 The reference is to the (in)famous *Smartavicharam* (the ritualized trial of Malayali Brahmin women accused of adultery and breach of seclusion) of an *Antharjanam* (Brahmin woman) called Kuriyedattu Tatri in the early twentieth century, who named sixty-five men from different castes, including the scions of high Brahmin aristocracy, in the 'trial'. In this case, the accused men were allowed to question her, but none of them could prove innocence, within the norms of Smarthavicharam. All sixty-five were excommunicated, along with her. The trial created quite a furore. For details of *Smartavicharam*, see Innes and Evans 1951 (1908): 383–84

13 Male head of the tarawad.

7

Mrs. K. Kannan Menon

Mrs. K. Kannan Menon, her married name, was what Edattatta Rugmini Amma often used in her articles. She was born in Talasherry, North Kerala, and was the first young woman to be educated in a convent there. She was well versed in Sanskrit and Malayalam literature, and had a remarkable command over English. She married her cousin Kappana Kannan Menon, who was a prominent figure in Nair reformism, closely associated with the formation of the Nair Service Society. Her major publications were articles in the women's magazine Lakshmibhayi, *run by Vellaikkal Narayana Menon, and appeared throughout the 1910s, many of which were replies and rejoinders of remarkable force. She died quite young, in the 1920s. She is reported to have written verses in English, which however have remained unpublished.*

'Modern Women and Their Husbands': A Rejoinder

It was while reading the essay with the above title in the past issue of the *Mahilaratnam*[1] that I became enlightened about the widespread existence of the eternal marital maladies described in it, even in this day and age. Nevertheless, are all women infected by the evils portrayed in that article? May they be held responsible for the situation?

The first charge raised by the author, M. Krishna Menon, against modernized young women is that 'they have begun to abandon social mores completely'. Among human beings, no one in their right senses will simply abandon all social mores. They may give up older ones and adopt new practices. But this method is not limited to young women. Such practice, adopted by young men and all other human beings in this world, is the way of the world, even if not its justice. The further misdeeds detected by the author are that these women harbour deep contempt and revulsion towards their husbands, and do not 'respect' them. Is this true? There has never been a time in which all young women hated their husbands, and there never will be. However, if some women do, there may be good reasons for it.

In our midst, marriages are not usually conducted with the consent of women or in their interest. If the father or the *karanavan*[2] manages to catch hold of some chap somehow, then marriage will soon follow. Often one does not even know whether the person one is supposed to wed is good-natured or otherwise, good-looking or not, and so on. A woman's duty is to be present at the fixed hour of marriage in the prearranged place, and then to suffer all the harassment, privation and frustration caused by that husband.

Sometimes, a girl barely stepping into youth is married off to a middle-aged man, without a twinge of reluctance. Besides, in many instances, the husband may be ignorant and unpolished in many respects, while the wife may be a woman of some education. It will indeed be a great surprise if the wife does not feel repelled by his inferior company and talk.

The other thing is respect. Now, everyone ought to realize that this is something that cannot be obtained through chiding, entreating, or at a price. The sense of respect for another arises when one perceives in the other a valuable quality that one does not possess, or one is incapable of possessing. This holds good for all irrespective of sex. Few Indians do not revere Sarojini Naidu or Mrs. Gandhi [Kasturba Gandhi]. If a person has an intrinsically venerable quality, no one will dishonour it. Men who wake up in the morning to ferret out petty inconveniences, work themselves into a rage over them, throw a few tantrums, depart for work, return at midnight, spending the evening in gambling or booze, are not at all rare. Is it not useless for such men to tom-tom such complaints, and flash such passports like, 'I am not being respected; it doesn't matter what I do—the *Puranas* instruct women that the husband is God incarnate for them, even if he may be an insufferable grouch,' and so on?

Some qualities are acquired by each of us at birth as human beings. Intelligence is prominent among them. Siblings, brothers and sisters born to the same parents, do not display equal levels of intelligence. Sometimes the girls are found less intelligent than boys; sometimes, the reverse is the case. Mother Nature does not differentiate between the sexes in this regard; she does not discriminate in favour of one over the other. However, the usual practice is to try to expand the minds of men through education; as for women's minds, they either remain in the same condition, or attain some development naturally. Irrespective of all the proofs of success, or degrees a man may amass, it is quite unlikely that a naturally level-headed and intelligent woman will respect him. Likewise, a woman will not respect a man for his good looks or wealth alone. Steadfastness of mind and a worthy character are what everyone admires. Husbands who lack such admirable qualities, but are dearly loved by their wives, and husbands who are not loved with such earnestness, but still command the respect and devotion of their wives, are quite commonplace. Marriage becomes beautiful and enjoyable when immaculate mutual love and respect commingle in it. However, this is rarely the case. The goodness and badness of the partners normally determine the amount of love and respect elicited.

Another of Mr. Menon's declarations goes like this: 'The husband is God Manifest.' He claims that this is laid down by the Shastras. Does the author himself go by other such Shastras? The Shastras propound the *varnasrama dharma*. Should we not observe them? Since we are said to be Shudras,[3] are not the knowledge of letters forbidden to us? Now let us see how much Godly Essence may be detected in the husband. The *Purana*s and the *Smriti*s have thought up thirty-three crores of Gods for the convenience of the Malayalis, who have no rule or tie in marriage.[4] If one marries a penniless God today, one may accept a well-to-do God tomorrow. If that God proves sickly, one may seek a healthy God the next day. If that too reveals any flaw, there is every provision to pursue another God who would fit the need. Convincing today's women of the principle which upholds that two people born of the same womb, growing up for some time under similar conditions, will transmogrify suddenly, one into God and the other into a weakling (*abala*), is quite a formidable task. The author contends that 'defying the wishes of the husband will bring forth the wrath of Gods.' When God is Man, it cannot possibly be otherwise.

'Women should spend their youth subservient to husbands, in obedience to them.' Indeed! What does this mean? Is it that at the end of youth, Man's power over Woman will dissipate? Or, does it mean that Woman will be liberated in this phase of the bondage she suffers as a wife?

Mr. Menon argues that 'any matter will shape up well only in the presence of a [male] Leader [nayakan]'. Will not a female leader [nayika] suffice? Madame Blavatsky who founded the new religion of Theosophy, Annie Besant who is now the President of that Society, Mrs. Pankhurst and her daughters who have fought valiantly for the entry of women into the English Parliament, Madame Krupp who heads the factory that produces the huge German guns that have impeded the soldiers of England, France and Russia alike—all of them are women. Even if delicate, who can establish that they all lack efficiency?

Matrimony is a crucial phase in human life. We know that it is not merely a human invention, as we see that any living thing displays the eagerness to unite with its mate. Since the human being is endowed with special intelligence, it demands certain specific qualities of its companion, and is either satisfied or dissatisfied at the presence or absence in its mate. Women with caring and devoted husbands who support them by their labour are not rare today. Such women serve their husbands with deep affection and devotion, are willing to launch into anything for their sake, and recognize that making their husbands comfortable is their responsibility. No woman is in need of the advice that she should heed and love her husband. This is the first lesson learned by the Womanly Heart from Nature. Every young girl at the threshold of youth begins to desire a bridegroom. Each one shapes a Manly model according to her understanding and character, and then wishes to see it personified in her husband. If these fantasies and desires come true, the woman rises to deserve the status of the wife, and fulfils her responsibilities ably and well. If not, she will defile that worthy rank.

Just as there are lechers among men, there will be a few harlots among women. Their husbands, who lack the mental strength to discipline them by stern words, should not proceed to decide that all women are similarly evil-natured or wanton. My only request is that such articles that vilify all women should not appear in this monthly, which bears such an exquisite name.

From 'Adhunikavanitaratnangalum Avarude Bharttakkanmarum: Oru Pratyakhyanam', *Mahilaratnam*, 1, 5, M.E. 1091 Dhanu (Dec–Jan 1915–16): 104–07.

Notes

1   This is a rejoinder to M. Krishna Menon Kanayannur's article of this name which appeared in *Mahilaratnam*, 1, 4, M.E. 1091 Vrischikam (Nov–Dec 1915): 85–88.
2   See Essay 6, n13.

3   Raises the idea, widespread in early twentieth-century reformism in Kerala, that the systems of marital alliances under matrilineal family arrangements were 'lawless', which happens to be prevalent in popular discourse even to this day. Often this perception was related to the observation that these systems were quite unlike patrilineal monogamous conjugal arrangements, deemed 'civilized' and 'moral'. For recent perspectives on this idea, see Kodoth 2001. The Nairs were counted as Shudras in the varna system of caste in Kerala.

8

K. M. Kunhulakshmy Kettilamma

K. M. Kunhulakshmy Kettilamma (1877–1947) was born in Kottayam, in Malabar, and was a scholar in Sanskrit and Malayalam. Her major work in Sanskrit was Prarthananjali. *Among her Malayalam books were* Savitrivrittam Puranachandrika *and* Kausalyadevi. *She edited the women's magazine,* Mahilaratnam.

Literature and Womankind

Literature means vigour', a learned scholar from the West is said to have declared so. It must be admitted that this idea is both interesting and lucid. A precondition for the utilization of any energy is that we must take into consideration its inclination and configuration. In the case of literary expression too, we need to show deference to certain important features. Literary work that is meaningless, that is, devoid of righteous intentions and sagacity, must not be allowed to blaze for long—in the same way that baneful energy must not be allowed to persist for long. It is this that puts literature and energy on common ground. Therefore, the watchful eyes of aspiring writers should always be focused upon the core elements of their activity, and the obligations involved, so that it does not deteriorate into futile exercises.

It is readily perceptible that menfolk take precedence in almost all varieties of ordered human activity in the cultured world. This tremendous expansion has been made possible by the multi-faceted power of freedom available to men and the refinement of the mind that it makes possible. There may not be many who hold male and female temperaments to be fundamentally different. The respective temperaments of men and women become distanced from each other through the distinct sorts of worldly affairs with which they come to, or are likely to come to, contact, as they attain maturity. If the growth in the intelligence of women and men engaged in the study of the same topics in the same school are compared, women may not excel men in performance. However, most people would agree that women attain the same levels as men. Thus it is the absence of like conditions that direct women and men into their distinctly different paths.

In a particular society, the epoch in which both women and men devote themselves to the pursuit of success in a spirit of equality may be counted as heralding the pinnacle of its civilization. It is then that life becomes pleasurable and plentiful for society as a whole, since the several worldly difficulties that plague the present scheme of living will vanish altogether. We must work together persistently and intelligently to accomplish this ultimate state of well-being.

Great men of different epochs have argued that 'the civilisation of a society ought to be measured by the refinement of education attained by its womenfolk'. It is not news that the status of women in modern Western nations is exceptionally high. Likewise, the distressingly vast difference between India and the Western nations in this regard is also not unknown to us. If the women of Kerala were to strive purposefully to further their social efforts, then the land of Kerala would step into the threshold of a remarkably fortunate era. Literature is foremost among the fields in which our sisters should toil with renewed vitality.

Women need to focus upon many factors in their efforts to claim for themselves a permanent niche in the literary field. Ill thought-out projects are bound to be rejected by society in the long run, however talented their proponents might be. Among these, the exertions of women, who lack sufficient worldly experience, are easily dissipated. If the women of Kerala are to make their mark in the literary field, then, first, they must demand social freedom, and win it through persistent struggle. It may be stated at the outset that to demand the same sort of freedom enjoyed by men for women does not suit our national ethos. This merely means that women should not be allowed unbounded freedom under all circumstances. If men invite women's cooperation and help in efforts to improve the condition of society, they will achieve success early. There are many instances that illustrate the mind's refinement through freedom. Literary efforts, especially, are fully dependent on genuine, self-acquired experience. This sort of experience is not available to women today. The freedom enjoyed by men endows all their endeavours with strength. The restrictions on women's freedom are responsible for the infrequency of their efforts. They must possess at least the social freedom that will permit them to reshape, classify and refine experience. How can any effort that relies upon indirect experience, that has not the strength derived from delving into the labyrinthine complexities, the twists and turns of the ways of the world, prove fecund? Mental faculties develop only when there is freedom of action. Is it not said that 'action influences the intelligence, but the intelligence does not influence action'?[1] If women are granted some more social freedom, they may enter the world of literature without much difficulty.

Along with social freedom, women will need help from men, and gradually, this must be replaced by their cooperation. Men have to help women in many ways until the experiences of women gain 'height and weight'. Without this, they may lose their bearing or self-control in the tangles of a complex world—once they have gained enough experience, they will be able to survive without much dependence on others—here, the responsibility of men would be to strive along with them on an equal plane.

Women possess many natural qualities that can embolden them to embark upon literary endeavours successfully. They may readily acquire virtuous causes, which is the primary requirement for enduring literature. Womanliness and innocence are not very distant. They are mutually entwined. Women's ideas incline naturally towards innocence.

Besides, the Womanly Heart is vested with far more tenderness than the Mind of Man. It is this single quality that is the exquisite seed of Compassion, or Love of one's Fellow Beings, which has inspired much captivating and mastery work. The works of Western poets have illustrated well how inspiring Compassion can be in literary expression.

Impartial lovers of literature are saddened by the fact that despite all its intrinsic greatness, the Womanly Heart has not been appropriately moulded. A few Great Women, here and there, have given us reason for relief that the women of Kerala are indeed capable of efforts to enrich the language. Once that relief is transformed into courage, and gradually forged into experience, we may indisputably rejoice that the inauspicious days of Malayalam [Kerala Bhasha] are indeed in the past. Honored Sisters! Let us all strive together so that such happy times may soon arrive.

From 'Streekalum Sahityavum', *Mahilaratnam*, 1, 3, M. E.1091 Tulam (Oct–Nov 1915): 50–52.

Note

1   *Karmanabadhyate Buddhir Buddhyaakarma Na Badhyate.*

9

Sarojini

This is probably a pen name of Edattata Rugmini Amma (see 7, this volume). The style and the concerns are strikingly similar to her other articles, which frequently appeared in journals in the second decade of the twentieth century. This was suggested to me by her granddaughter, who also pointed out that her daughter's name was Sarojini.

Womanliness

Everyone knows what Manliness is. However, even those who lecture or write about Womanliness do not seem to have thought deeply about what Womanliness is. It is quite doubtful whether everyone will supply the same answer if asked to make a list of the virtues that ought to grace a woman ideally. The author of the *Nitisara* jotted down the list of Womanly virtues in the shloka that begins with '*Karyeshu mantri, Karaneshu dasi* . . .'[1] The sage Kanva's solemn reflections on the ideal attributes of the homemaker have been interred in the verse that begins '*Bhaktya sevika poojyan* . . .'[2] The features found necessary by the one are not demanded by another. That 'another' may requisition some other traits in addition, or 'by order'. If the ideal, genteel and virtuous wife (*kuladharnmapatni*) must necessarily resemble the Goddess of Prosperity in looks (*rupeshu Lakshmi*), then what are all the inauspicious-creatures (*moodhevikal*) to do, except nullify themselves through poison, or get married into ill-bred families? Certainly, there would have been a point if it had been demanded that women should acquire all virtues securable through human effort. If impossible cravings leave one frustrated, who is to be reproached, except one's own unjustified cupidity? If men do not have a steady opinion as to what merits are essential for the ideal woman, how are women to know what they must get in order to gratify them? Instability is, of course, another word for fickleness. Is fickleness a male quality or a female one? The *Nitisara* provides excellent documentary evidence to show that though 'fickle' [*chapala*], the virgin's mind is really set upon a single wish. Men cannot argue that they demand too much. The father demands knowledge of the bridegroom, the mother demands wealth, and the relatives demand high birth. The virgin demands only good looks.[3] And she is fixed on that. Yet ugly men are forever ready to enter the tournament to win the hand of the bride! The Creator will have to embark upon fresh creation to shape men who will not bow low before a high-hat of a princess. It is quite doubtful whether there are any men who have not consulted the Rx [a medical symbol] of Vidura's antipyretic syrup (*shadangu kashayam*) that prescribes 'men who sing, and men who dance'. [In the story of Devayani in the *Mahabharatam* in which Vidura talks of women's partiality towards men who dance and sing.] All the scholars adore this brew. On listening to the necessity of being rupeshu Lakshmi, one may feel like decking up a bit. But the aphorism that 'the beautiful wife is but an enemy' (*Bharya rupavati shatru*) will be displayed at once to turn that enthusiasm into annoyance.

There will also be counsel against the craving for jewellery. Then in the very same breath, the precept that there can be no procreation without beautification will be quoted. Women and men need distinct precepts to guide eating, sleeping, and so on and on. The wife must eat only after the husband eats.

An early meal is prohibited even if one may faint of hunger. On the heels of this will come the translation of the English proverb that promises showers of gold from going to sleep early and rising early. Yet the shloka that warns the wife to sleep only after her husband has slept, will follow. In short, the ideal, genteel and virtuous wife is synonymous with she who sleeps less.

Now let us leave the shloka-spinners for the *Purana*-seekers. From reading the *Puranas* and the epics, it seems clear that their authors think that women should be eager to stomach any torment and endure any sorrow, and carry on under any circumstances. Sita suffered for twelve years, living in the forest with her husband. Then she suffered a year's separation at Ravana's abode. Soon after, she publicly entered the fire to prove that her sojourn in Ravana's house had not tarnished her. But even that proved insufficient to alleviate the suspicions of her husband and the people, and she was abandoned, fully pregnant and defenceless, in the forest. She, who should have given birth in the king's palace, delivered in the hermitage of a sage. The pain endured by a mother in bringing forth and raising a child, even with help from the husband and relatives, is immense. Without anyone's help, Sita gave birth to twins and nurtured them.

Chandramati was a queen. To fulfil an absurd promise made by her husband, she sold herself and her son. Mother and son slaved in housework. She pounded paddy until her hands bled in the house of the Brahmin who had bought her. Yet the benevolent master allowed her to catch a glance of her son, dead of a cobra's bite in the forest, only at midnight.

Savitri was a princess. She wed Satyavan in her heart. Satyavan had no money, no house to live anywhere in the land. He had blind parents to care for in the forest. Despite all this, she took him as her husband in her heart, considering nothing but his virtue. The great sage Narada chided her, prophesying her widowhood, as Satyavan would be short-lived. Her father tried to dissuade her, too. Savitri argued that the heart could not fall in love with two people in one lifetime, and went ahead to marry him. The day of Satyavan's death drew close. The God of Death approached with his staff and rope. But the radiance of Savitri's chastity kept him at bay. I will not elaborate further. Savitri propitiated the God of Death to win back Satyavan's life, and many other boons. She thus revealed to the world the power and the purity of love.

Seelavathi's chastity and virtue are a cut above all this. That noble woman's husband was Ugratapas, who would never relent, even before the most devout, sustained attention and care. Besides, he was also an awful leper, with fingers falling off to reveal worms and pus within, to the utter revulsion of the onlookers. But that chaste wife would eat only his leftovers as if it were *panchamritam*,[4] and that too, only after reverently removing the fallen finger from the plate.

Some such stars as these have risen and set in the world of Womankind. This continues to happen today. They, however, dwindle and die, unnoticed by those who are eager only to espy ill-omened comets. The authors of the *Puranas* have thought up stories with situations so horrific and difficult that the imagination could be stretched no further, to offer examples of wifely chastity. What a terrible pity that the women of Kerala, who are forever reading, learning and imbibing these examples and praising the women of the *Puranas*, have earned nothing but the slander that the rule of chastity does not apply to them![5] Intelligent people should think over and decide whether they did really earn this, or whether this was a bogus legacy foisted upon them by men.

Yet, despite knowing well of the existence of such Jewels of Womanliness in the *Puranas*, many are still eager to proclaim in rhyming verse that women are frail (*abala*) and fickle (*chapala*). Even Sita's husband has certified that 'he who heeds the word of a woman is a total fool'. Non-capricious men are ever-enthusiastic about pouring scorn upon poor capricious women, and composing rhetorical verse on the possibility of the *Atti* tree bursting into bloom, the crow turning pearly, the fish growing legs, and the impossibility of stability in the Womanly heart. They would delight in delving into the meanings and establishing these as verily the Vedas. And of course, they are fully enlightened as to what Manliness is!

Men will insist with utmost seriousness that Womanliness consists of putting up with the insults of men, following their rules, bowing to them as though they were divinities, allowing them to do whatever they please, and patiently lugging along the burdens they impose, even when left abject and friendless by them. Beauty is a must, and besides the tresses of hair must be long and wavy. The curls on the forehead must gently dance even when there is no breeze to ruffle them. The eyes must be constantly animated, like the flutter of black-hued bees on a white lotus. The body must be as delicate as young shoots tender enough to wither in the sun. The complexion must be like either the bloom of the hibiscus, or the golden lemon. The waist must be so dainty that the onlooker would fear that it might not withstand the strain of standing up straight. The backside must be heavy enough for the ankle to make a dimple in fine sand while walking on it. If all this can be written down in rhyming verse, the Great Poet, he who has described the City, the Ocean, the Mountain and the Seasons (*Nagararnavashailatrtukaran Mahakavi*) will be satisfied. The playwright will not be averse to making the chivalrous hero pine away behind the trees, if blue blood can be counted amongst his characteristics. If the pining comes before, and knowledge of the blue blood later, the guiding precept 'in doubtful cases, the state of the mind is the rule' is available always. The novelists will be mollified with the B.A. exam, the blouse and the half-sari. They are not so insistent upon blue blood. There are numerous precedents to draw upon—like the blindness and the deafness of love. Today we see enough of the speeding up of the mail train so that the aristocratic girl may elope with the beggar, and its derailing through the breaking of the shoe of the mount upon which the girl's guardian was hurrying to seek them out. All emanating from novelists who have fully grasped the Achilles' Heel of Love. Let the poets and the playwrights describe Womanliness as lodged in all this. If poets, novelists and their adoring and compliant readership fail to see that Womanliness does not abide in a body that melts like fresh butter in the labour room of a noble mansion, in silk from China, upper-cloths from Kottar, or diplomas from universities, at least other women ought to recognize it.

Women are not in a position to ask men to stop insulting them; nor can they return the compliments. Let us pray to God that men themselves develop the charity to stop the slurs at least now. Human beings have some distinct qualities that set them apart from animals. These constitute humanness. Though women and men ought to have these equally, women have proved that they are not only equal, but also definitely superior to men in this regard, through firm and just acts.

Love is a virtue that refines humanness. This character is not seen in men with the same intensity with which it is seen in women. Even men will not venture to argue that they can rival women in affection for parents, siblings and relatives. If one claims that the love for children is ten times stronger in mothers compared to fathers, it may appear a bit rhetorical. 'Twice' will settle any difference of opinion: only half of the father's property has been made available to the children through reform.[6] But the whole of the mother's property will go to no one but the children, reform or no reform. On entering the husband-wife relationship, men's hesitation seems unremitting. The United Companies of Sanskrit scholars have cast and amassed several cannons of high-sounding verse to pulverize the forts that protect women, like the prescription of the five *ashramas* for men, and none for women. Sriraman and the common folk remained sceptical despite the fact that Sita was made to jump into a pyre to prove that she had not been desecrated by her stay in Ravana's dwelling. Urmila, however, had no hesitation, though Lakshmanan had stayed away for twelve years and indeed, had gone berserk all over Surpanakha's nose and other parts, like a tipsy toddy-tapper on a coconut tree. Seelavathi bore a leper on her shoulders to a courtesan's house to do his bidding. She performed excruciating austerities to see that the sun would not rise up unless that mighty sorehead, who had died on the way, was given back to her. The so-very-non-fickle minds of men who put together the Regulation[7] that women should have but one husband, proved too cowardly to also dictate that a man should have but one wife. Yet the high-sounding Sanskrit cannons are directed at poor women alone.

To say that women are superior to men in their love for relatives may not convince the author of the '*Panchatantra* of the Mother-in-Law'. The mantra to restore the peace of mind of the daughter-in-law vanquished in the struggle with the mother-in-law goes thus: 'Place the mother-in-law,/Upon the grinding-stone,/And then with another stone . . . Narayana!'[8]

Mahakavi Valmiki has missed out on an important link in the *Ramayanam*. Our *Sitadukham*[9] is of course the result of an attempt at correction made by a Malayali (male) expert in wranglings caused by mothers-in-law. Who does not feel irked by mother-in-law, Kausalya, and the junior mothers-in-laws, who caused Sita such misery? It is difficult not to admit that women too have some blame to bear as far as squabbles between sisters-in-law are concerned. As with love, it can also be proved that women are a cut above men in virtues like compassion, generosity, and so on. If there is something like mildness in the human heart, it certainly belongs to the Womanly Heart.

> '*The heart of ideal Men*
> *Looks harder than the diamond*
> *Yet more delicate than the tender bud*
> *To think of it—who knows?*'

Even Mahakavi Bhavabhuti has no clue about the situation in Manly Hearts.[10] Yet everyone finds the decree about 'Woman's Heart' (*streenamcha chittam*) (being fickle) palatable.[11] Though the precept is that 'Even the Gods cannot know the hearts of women',[12] even the street-brats are made to sing of their fickleness! Myth and history reveals men fighting and losing their lives in their lust for women. However, there is neither myth nor history to testify that women have at least bickered over men. Women must remain so till the end of time. That is Womanliness.

From 'Streetvam', *Mahilaratnam*, 1, 5, M. E. 1091 Dhanu (Dec–Jan 1915–16): 97–102. The same article with the same title appeared signed by 'Oru Stree' (A Woman) in *Mahila*, 13, 2, 1933: 33–36.

Notes

1 According to Sarnghadhara's version of this in *Sarnghadhara Paddhati*, the ideal wife was to be like a minister in practical affairs, like a menial in service, like the Goddess of Prosperity in appearance, like a mother in affection, and like a courtesan in bed.
2 From A. R. Rajaraja Varma's *Sakuntalam*, in which the sage Kanva advises his foster-daughter Sakuntala, about to begin her journey to her husband's palace, of wifely duty. He advises her to worship revered persons with devotion, to consider her co-wives to be sisters, to be pleasant to her husband, even if he may not be so, to be merciful to servants and not to turn haughty in good fortune. He reminds her that if the homemaker did not confirm to this, she would be a pestilence.
3 This too refers to a Sanskrit shloka from the *Nitisastras*, which specifies what specific qualities are demanded of the bridegroom by different members of the bride's party.
4 A mixture of ripe banana, honey, jaggery, clarified butter and grapes, given to devotees as blessings from temples.
5 Obviously refers to the matrilineal marital arrangements, in which the tie of marriage was not considered to be necessarily binding for life, though the degree of freedom allowed to the woman in choosing a partner or divorcing him, could vary very considerably. It also entailed that the children born out of wedlock had little formal claims over the father's wealth. For a detailed account, see Schneider and Gough 1961.

6 The reference must be to the First Nair Regulation of 1912 of Tiruvitamkoor, which decreed that half of a man's property must go to his own children.
7 A reference, again, to the First Nair Regulation, 1912, which had the provision to prosecute a Nair woman if she accepted another man as husband while still being married to another. However, in the discussion preceding the Second Nair Regulation of 1925, it was strongly argued that polygamy must also be ended. There was, indeed, an influential group that argued in favour of a certain qualified sort of polygamy. The arguments of both supporters and opponents are summarized in the *Malayala Manorama*'s report on the proceedings of the Shree Mulam Popular Assembly, dated 12 June 1924. See also, Saradamoni 1999.
8 This is from Karyatt Achyuta Menon's *Ammayipanchatantram* (The Panchatantra of the Mother-in-Law), which was a popular work that lampooned matriliny.
9 A song usually sung in accompaniment to the *kaikottikkali* dance performed by women on festive-ritual occasions, which relates an episode of the folk version of the *Uttaramacharitam*, in which Sita falls prey to the machinations of her mothers-in-law, who persuade her to draw a picture of Ravana as if to satisfy their innocent curiosity, and then use it against her before Rama.
10 This is a shloka from Bhavabhuti's *Uttararamacharitam*.
11 The well-known shloka that says that the leaping of the horse, the sounding of thunder, the movement of women's hearts, the direction of men's fortunes, and the increase or decrease in rainfall remain unpredictable, unknown even to the Gods, and therefore to men.
12 The reference is to the shloka mentioned in n11.

10

B. Pachi Amma

This author is not known otherwise, but it is likely that this name was a pseudonym for B. Bhageeraty Amma, who edited The Mahila, *one of the most important women's journals in early twentieth-century Kerala. Not only is 'Pachi' the usual pet name for 'Bhageeraty', but also the style of writing bears uncanny similarity to her writings.*

Women and Freedom
(Part One)

Good heavens! Many eyes will redden, many faces will be etched with deep frowns, upon seeing these two words written together! Many may decide to reject the article without reading it or indeed, fling down the magazine in a huff. I would like humbly request such readers to resort to such imprudent acts only after reading the whole article.

The present inhabitants of Kerala are of different sorts. There is one group that hangs on obstinately to the injunction 'Woman deserves no freedom' (*Na Stree Swatantryamarhati*) and keep muttering under their breath that 'all of today's women are hankering after freedom. This is the sign of the *Kaliyug*. This is the beginning of the end', and so on. Another group claims that 'woman *already* possesses virtuous freedom. They should not be allowed anymore. Today's *poisonous* education makes them *averse* to marital ties. The world is beginning to decay.' So goes their argument. There are also some cultivated minds, which cherish pride in the their nation and their community, and maintain that women should be granted their just measure of liberty. Of these, the first two are not very different. Reckoning that an outright and obstinate rejection of women's liberty may impoverish their 'modern' credentials, they [the members of the second group] merely reiterate their conservatism in different terms. Leave this as it is. What position did the wise Indians of ancient times grant women? Will women be allowed freedom? If yes, let us carefully consider the matters in which it may be permitted.

It is surely an unblemished truth that the ancient Indians were wiser. It may be readily proved that they allowed women rightful freedom and worshipped them appropriately. Marriage is a rite of equal importance for Woman and Man. Merely ponder what freedom our ancestors granted women in this matter. *Gandharva Vivaham* [secret marriage of lovers] and *Swayamvaram* [marriage of choice] were permitted in those times. This was not because our ancestors were ignorant; rather, it stemmed from their superior intelligence. They understood well that in marriage, the mutual compatibility and the consent of the bride and the groom matter the most. The secret of the durability of marital ties in those times lies precisely in this. The women of those days had the right to divorce their husbands. Their advice was considered valuable. Their freedom of opinion was not curtailed. Many even volunteered to fight in battles. Sriparameshwaran's androgynous form as *Ardhanariswara*, and the eminence he granted to Ganga Devi are, of course, excellent illustrations of the high status enjoyed by women in those times.

What about the condition of women in modern times? Describing it as despicable a thousand times over will not suffice. Women are not allowed to express their opinions even in the weighty matter of marriage. In this affair, they are little above lifeless objects of exchange. How pathetic! More than three-fourths of one's life is to be spent in matrimony. It is claimed, indeed, that women should not realize this; that they should not seek to make matrimony comfortable! In most communities in Kerala (no, really, in all communities) custom dictates that women must have no recourse but to wed the men chosen by their guardians. Even if the prospective husband is an ignorant boor, a leper, a drunkard, or a philanderer, a Malayali woman has no right to alter even an inch the decision taken by her parents or elders. Worse, she cannot even voice her grievance (it may be admitted that there are refined persons who would rebel against such control. But an opinion can be formed only through considering the state of the majority). What further example will one need to make evident the lack of liberty of women in the present? Bhageeraty Amma's declaration in the first issue of *The Mahila* that wives do not possess even the minimal right to inquire about their husbands' destinations when they go out, is not an exaggeration at all.[1] Among a hundred persons, at least ninety-five or more insist that women have been created for working in the kitchen and reproduction, and conduct their lives in the light of this notion, even in this twentieth century, nay, even in this month of March 1921, when the Sun of Progress is believed to have reached its apogee. Given this, if the call for the right to liberty rings aloud within the world of the women of Kerala, they have certainly not striven for it. Why be astonished at this? Why be envious? Why be angry?

Men alone do not make a community. It can be formed only by women and men together. Thus it is definite that when we speak of the prosperity of the community, we refer to the prosperity of both sexes. How can the community prosper if men alone secure education and culture, and women carry on like poultry promised to the oven, or, alternately, like yogis tending the sacred fire in sacrifices, or like cats that skulk around kitchens?

If the Westerners had hung fast to this particular mulishness characteristic of the people of Kerala, where would be they now? Who took up most of the responsibilities left behind by men fighting the war? Women.[2] If Kerala faces such an exigency—God forbid—will our women be useful in any way? What will be their plight, when the guns start booming? Why should this be so? If their cowardice makes good-for-nothings out of them, who is responsible for that? Men, of course. If women have become sluggish, it is because they have been shut up in kitchens. To cut it short, a fair share of liberty must be bequeathed to womenfolk.

Now I have something to say about the term *swatantryam*.[3] In the earlier issue,[4] Vatakkumkur Rajaraja Varma,[5] a respected friend, wrote: 'It is quite improper that women are interpreting the idea of *swatantryam* in an unacceptable way and yearning for it.' Indeed, it would be most improper if someone sought to misinterpret the concept and pursue distorted goals. Indeed, I would go as far as to condemn such effort as a heinous act that must be averted at once. But my firm belief is that not even one of my educated Malayali sisters has taken, or will take, such a direction. The respected Raja continues: 'Women have already gained enough of virtuous freedom by now. It is far better not to have the freedom to wander alone in parks, visit theatres, dance, and become slaves to wage labour and paid employment, like the white females.' Here I am assailed by several doubts. First, I do not understand the meaning he ascribes to 'virtuous freedom' [*satvika swatantryam*]. I also do not see what may constitute the lack of freedom. To turn the demand for liberty advanced by the women of Kerala into the dancing, the strolling-in-parks and the theatre-attendance of Western women, whose ideals of life are entirely unlike [ours], is definitely a foolhardy thing to do. I do not think that any Malayali sister who asks for liberty will desire all that. There are many able ladies in Kerala today who have passed the higher examinations and struggle for the freedom of women. I have also come to know with pride that many of them hail from my community. We also know of the way of life of many such women. Yet none of them desire the above-mentioned abandon. Do desist from assessing women by the same standards of change that seem to have guided today's men. According to the respected Raja's designs, women ought to appease themselves with what he believes to exist, that is, 'virtuous freedom', which is nothing other than the modern condition I described earlier. God alone knows how many will consent to this.

Asking us to be wary of wage labour is certainly a bit of salutary advice. This only means that women should not remain subject to status quo. More so because women today are slaves of wage labour; but in ordinary wage labour, the wages are fixed. Here, the only difference is that this is not the case. Our sisters are mainly occupied with work related to the kitchen. The wages are set by the husband's munificence—no, indeed—by his benevolence. Another statement made by the Raja appears quite opaque. 'The poisonous education prevalent today makes women abhor the ties of marriage, just like the men.' One does not know whether this statement is true. I am willing to concede that the current system of education is utterly defective. However, I do not agree that it makes women apathetic to wedlock. If they do indeed display inhibition, some other reason must be sought. He [the Raja] states that marriage, once sublime and exalted in our lives, has become a bouncing ball providing ample entertainment for lawyers and judges in courts—he must be referring to the rare *samari* cases,[6] or suits for divorce. Actually, the Raja's statement is evidence that upholds the necessity of giving women freedom and making men more responsible and moral. For women file for maintenance because their husbands have not been caring, because their husbands have heartlessly abandoned them. If women are filing for divorce, that is because they were given no say in their marriages, and because the grooms' eligibility was never seriously assessed. Therefore, if marriage has become the bouncing ball of the judiciary, the fault does not lie with women. All that has been said here about the Raja's article is merely incidental; my article is not a rejoinder to it.

From 'Streekalum Swatantryavum (Bhagam 1)', *The Mahila*, 1, 3 (March 1921): 108–13.

Notes

This essay may have been in more than one part; however, I have been able to find only Part One.

1   The reference is to B. Bhageeraty Amma, the editor of *The Mahila*. For biographical note, see Essay 21, 'Women and Literature', this volume.
2   The reference is to British women's active role during World War I.
3   In strict terms, the word means 'self-means for survival', though it is often used to mean 'freedom' in a loose sense.
4   Vatakkumkur Rajaraja Varma Raja, 'Mahilamahatmyam', *The Mahila* 1, 2, 1921: 48–52.
5   Vatakkumkur Rajaraja Varma (1891–1970) was a much-revered Sanskrit scholar, poet and author, whose *Keraleeyasam-skritasahityacharitram* (The History of Sanskrit Literature in Kerala) is a highly-valued work. His other works include *Raghuveeravijayam*, *Uttarabharatam*, *Raghavaabhyudayam* and *Kerala Sahitya Charitram*. He was the Chief Pandit of the Oriental Manuscripts Library under the government of Tiruvitamkoor for some time, and later, a member of the Kochi Language Reform Committee, and of the Kerala Sahitya Akademi. He has some thirty books to his credit, and was awarded several titles like *Mahakavi*, *Kavitilakan*, *Sahityaratnam* and *Vidyabhooshanam*.
6   This refers to cases to be tried without much formal procedure or delay. *Samari* originates from the English word 'summary'.

11

K. Padmavaty Amma

The author wrote very frequently in Lakshmibhayi *in the early decades of the twentieth century. Other details, however, are not known.*

Malayali Marriage Modified

> *The damsels, they run, they hide,*
> *Seeing the man with beard all gray.*[1]

In those days, it seems shaving was not as common as it is now. If it had been common, then Seelavathi's husband wouldn't have been so aggrieved. Poor man—he ought to have lived in this twentieth century. Now, the graying of the beard isn't a problem at all. All you have to do is shave regularly. Finish it off before six o'clock in the morning. Besides, if you are somewhat well off, then the graying of the beard, or the hair, or even the loss of teeth—none of these will ever be a problem. In these days, there is no difficulty at all to get young 'damsels'. They won't flee or hide; indeed, they will chase you at a frantic pace. How astonishing! Shaving will solve the gray beard; what about the gray hair? Well, well, that's nothing. Even young people have gray hair at times. The teeth . . . what to do about that? No problem—spend a few rupees on first class false teeth! You have only to be careful at night. Even young people who don't have pretty enough teeth knock them off for better ones. Then what's the hitch about others whom God himself has favoured?

In our midst, those who resemble Seelavathi's husband are enjoying a lucky spell. People have lost all compunction about sacrificing young and nubile girls to graybeards in their autumn years. If 'the man be young and the woman old' is changed to 'the woman be young and the man be old', will not the effect be the same? As Damayanti remarks [in the *Nalacharitam*], 'Will they ever feel a little of love, will they ever be at peace, is there a greater disaster?' But such deep thinking is of no use these days. The last census, it seems, shows us that there are more women than men. And moreover, in reality do we not find many women who remain virgins right up to old age, never becoming wives, in Malayali families? In such a situation, will not the moustache receive an extra caress? Well, there are other reasons also for extended virginity of Malayali women (they are equally the reasons for the good fortune enjoyed by Ugratapas[2] and his breed).

A woman scholar has recommended that 'women must be wedded to handsome, generous and brave young men'. It is an open secret that if we proceed to look for 'young men' of this sort to wed our girls, there will be no end to our troubles. Among us—among the Hindus—there are few today who would have 'secret marriages for love' (*Gandharvam*), or the 'marriage of interiorities', as in *Indulekha*.[3] Let that be so. Even if we proceed in the well-trodden way to arrange an ordinary alliance, the first question asked by young men would be 'how much will they pay?' If he doesn't ask this straight, it will be asked through some go-between. The sums demanded will vary according to the financial situation of the parties involved. In the normal case, the list would be as below: For a common country bumpkin (this eligibility is quite well known to the person himself), a sum ranging from about two hundred to five hundred, may go up a bit according to paying capacity. This is fourth quality. The third-quality, some bit of English education and a job that fetches some ten or fifteen rupees monthly, the amount will be four-figured. It's enough to have a scent of English; there is no insistence on a proper knowledge of English. But the fellow must be able to manage to read and write his address in English. He must always sign his name in English. Shirt-Coat-Tie-Shoes must necessarily be used. These are all signs of English. Then we have the B.A. holders. They can be regarded as the second-class. Though the salary they would get if they aspired for employment in government is but a trifling sum, in marriage they are hard bargainers. It is accepted practice that the bidding for them should start from a thousand upwards, and there are no upper limits.

There is a special sub-section to this class. Some bright young chaps who pass B.A. don't even think of higher education until they manage to corner a marriage alliance. Seeking an alliance is a sure sign of hankering for higher education. The talk would then be over an agreement about a sum to cover the entire expenses of a B.L. degree, or an M.A., B.L. Not bad, is it? Is it not said, 'the wife is half the man?' Whatever had been attained till then came about through by one's own exertions. Even the *Puranas* say that the rest is the burden of the wife! It won't be too far off the mark if one said that the education of such characters is a major way in which people's money is unfairly and unnecessarily drained into the coffers of the government. This expense is largely useless; most of these chaps take off for Madras and Calcutta in the name of education and have a jolly time there.

Now for the members of the first-class. This class is constituted by those who have successfully surpassed all the obstacles mentioned before to settle into departments as officers or become lawyers. Since they excel all the others, their price, too, exceeds that of all the others. Ordinary folk needn't even think of them. Their needs are various. Some will be in debt; they need to clear up that; others will have pledged joint-family properties, and will want to recover them; yet others want to take some legal measures and seek to cover those expenses; some others will want to please their fathers or maternal uncles and will require to pay a sum for that; for some the same need will arise for the Karanavar. Not to say more, all the ways in which money can be extracted with appropriate excuses will be resorted to. To put it really flatly, today's men have unanimously passed the rule that plenty of money should be necessarily be made through the marital alliance. So, if a petition for marriage is filed by those who need it, the first matter taken up by them is that of the sum to be elicited. Once this section is elaborated to their satisfaction, everything is settled. The more important elements like appearance, youth, family and character would come up only afterwards. And these may not be considered at all. For, as far as all that is demanded by the woman's side is that the man should know English (as per status), and all that is demanded by the man's side is that some money should be made (that too, as per status), and as far as the man and woman involved are concerned, these remain the sole considerations, other things do not bother them. Anyway, well and good if they manage to strike a deal through shrewd bargaining; the very same if they split over the *sum* in question. This is the way in which all marriages are planned and conducted these days. The major rituals of this modified marriage include making promissory notes, legal bonds, documents, registration (I don't know if there are more) and arguments over these, and mediation in these matters.

My dear sisters! I have not failed to think what the intention of men must be in instituting such a system (I say that men instituted this because the insistence over the money is indeed theirs), and whom it benefits. You will be able to see on your own after some thought that they have not established this system without good reasons. What would you value more, something you buy at a price, or something that comes free? Which thing would you keep with utmost attention and care? Will you not be especially partial to the bought thing, and stay vigilant to keep it safe and sound? This is what men are demanding from you. Some may say, 'If men marry for money they will end up as slaves to women.' These are but justifications aimed at pulling the wool over the eyes of guileless womenfolk. Just think, who has the burden of *taking care* of the husband, if you buy him at a price? If you are not vigilant, your fate will be like that of the Brahmin in the tale of the Brahmin and his servant. If the servant goes so does the Brahmin's nose! What a pain in the neck! Like the poor Brahmin who had to put up with the burden of seeing that both the nose and the servant are not lost, the wife will have to bear the burden of seeing that the husband and the money paid, both are not lost! If these are lost by any chance, still, the loss is to the wife! If it is so very cumbersome to earn a first husband, do we need to labour on how difficult must it be to earn a second one? However we may try, the charge would be, 'it's second-hand stuff, and that's no good'. Like in trying to sell off a bicycle. However good the bicycle may be, if someone has used it, it's value shrinks.

Likewise a woman earns a first husband at considerable expense. Even if he, for some reason (quite possibly out of his lechery or foolishness), goes after another wife, the loss and the pain are all the woman's. If you ask if women reap no benefit at all from this practice, I would, well, agree, and say yes. If women have wealth of their own, or if their relatives are willing to spend liberally on them, they will have no reason to be disappointed. Only that they must be willing to spend enough money to secure a husband who would fit their specifications. In other words, to pick a husband from the agriculturists, the easy-livers, the employed or the self-earning, according to taste.

No one should protest that it is like cattle trading. Keen thought makes this appear pretty close to it, though. But can't we always opt not to state it so baldly? Anyway, women have a great deal to gain from private property. It's not enough that the taravad has property. Private property is something we can't do without. For that would endow everyone with husbands. Girls who have no wealth, that is, girls who have not the wherewithal to maintain a husband in style once they have got him, their cause can only be thought as gone for good. It's no use if these girls with no assets may have other good points. Irrespective of whether your looks are wonderful or terrible, irrespective of whether you know several languages and are well versed in music and the other arts, or whether you are an unlettered idiot, what matters is whether you can make a down payment. If you can't, then, hard luck! Why are you sad? The scriptures say that one attains spiritual salvation and worldly happiness in the service of one's husband. Is this easily possible? Is it a simple affair? So, why mourn over spending some money in a matter that would fetch you spiritual salvation and worldly happiness, that is, in the matter of attaining the status of a wife?

Among the major gains cornered by men through this system, firstly comes the gain in wealth, secondly, the gain of a wife, and thirdly, the special affection bestowed by such a wife: in case of ill-health, the special attention of the wife and even her family is fully guaranteed. Fourthly, if by some good luck the wife dies or if she is abandoned, one can once again go through the whole act and make even more money! These are the important advantages to be secured.

Alas, how unfortunate that shallow-minded human beings who alone have been blessed by God with the special ability to discern the mutual obligations of men and women, and their tasks and duties in marriage, must behave as the brutes in total disregard for good and evil! Can the practices of a people that have received even a modicum of culture and knowledge be so depraved? As long as each of you do not recognize your proper duties and discharge them well, will your community prosper? Or otherwise, if the Nairs had any love for their community, would they try to encourage such despicable practices? It is not surprising if such practices were fostered by people who had no education and culture, with no refinement of the intellect, and steeped in ignorance and darkness. But now things seem different. These detestable practices are being encouraged by those very people who claim to be sophisticated, and constantly put on airs as if they were striving to better the condition of the community in all ways. Is this worthy, indeed, of people of this sort?

The statements that follow are from an article written by my dear friend Cheruvari Rugmini Amma in the *Lakshmibhayi*.[4] Since they pertain to a matter that we women need to pay close attention to, I do believe that it will not be inappropriate to insert them here.

> 'If you do not find a bridegroom whom you like and is worthy of you, then it is much better to live either in the service of your parents who have cared for you and protected you from all difficulties, to earn divine blessings, or educate yourselves as much as your intelligence and situation will permit, to gain appropriate employment. In this way, to hang on to the foolish belief that wifehood alone encapsulates Womanly Duty, to bob about aimlessly in this Ocean of Worldliness full of worry, disease and want, and thus destroy one's life, in this universe that contains many different paths to hither-worldly happiness and other-worldly salvation, is nothing less than a great crime.'

Whatever be that, I would like to end this essay by placing before the people my humble opinion that it is necessary that this new sort of modified marriage in our midst must be either proscribed, or subjected to timely and suitable alterations.[5]

From 'Parishkritareetiyilulla Malayalivivaham', *Lakshmibhayi*, 9, 7, M.E. 1099 Tulam (Oct-Nov 1923–24): 231–47.

Notes

1 From the well-known Malayalam poet Kunjan Nambiar's *Seelavathicharitam*.
2 See Essay 2, n5.
3 *Indulekha* (1889) was O. Chandu Menon's well-known novel, one of the earliest in Malayalam, and it was a tale of romantic love between two modern-educated members of a matrilineal family, in which the couple are said to have been married 'in their hearts' long before they were formally united in the marital tie. For an interesting analysis of the notion of interiority in early modern Kerala see Udaya Kumar 1997.
4 Cheruvary Rugmini Amma, 'Vivaham' Part I, *Lakshmibhayi*, 3, 5, 1917–18: 191–96; Part II, *Lakshmibhayi*, 3, 6, 1918: 238–45. The quotation is from Part II: 244.
5 Indeed, later in the mid-twentieth century, the 'modification' of marriage among the matrilineal social groups would be depicted by K. Saraswati Amma in her short stories, with a precision and clarity rarely matched, even in social science research. See Devika 2003.

12

Vengalil K. Chinnammalu Amma

Vengalil K.Chinnammalu Amma (d. 1958) was the eldest daughter of a lawyer, Komath Krishna Kurup, and Vengalil Lakshmikutty Amma. She hailed from Panniyankara, near Kozhikode in north Kerala and spent her childhood at Talashery, but lived most of her adult life as a single woman in Chennai (Madras), as a teacher and social worker. The well-known diplomat and former Defence Minister of India, V. K. Krishna Menon, was her brother. In her memoir of V. K. Krishna Menon, his grandniece writes of her grandaunt thus: 'Chinnammalu Amma was a woman of rare brilliance, who had by the age of 14, had authored her first book. She had the unique experience of appearing for a public examination in which her book was the text of the syllabus. After the death of their mother, the reins of the house at Tellichery were offered to Chinnammalu Amma. She was, however, not interested in anything domestic, but spent all her time either reading or writing. She was proficient in Malayalam, Sanskrit, English, French and Latin and wrote articles and essays in all these languages.' (Ram 1997: 3–4)

The Place of Women in Society

One of the surest measures of the excellence of a society is the position women occupy in it. Western savants and our ancient preceptors are agreed upon this. Besides, emergent conditions and directions in the world too are moving towards this view of things. The great patriot Lala Lajpat Rai records in his reminiscences of travel in America that the womenfolk of America have contributed more to the advancement of that society than the menfolk. There, women are far more assiduous. In the *Puranas* and the epics we do see a society in which women enjoyed full freedom. A comparison with the present, however, would reveal that we ought to be ashamed even to claim descent from those women. The idea that women have no authority to enter matters relevant to the world outside their homes was nonexistent in ancient India. That was a belief, a malignant force, which spread in society during our dark times: In the *Mahabharatam* did not Kunti and Draupadi have opinions regarding the war? When Lord Krishna set forth as the messenger of the Pandavas, did not an impassioned Draupadi argue vehemently against a compromise? We do not see Krishna or the Pandavas interrupting her on the grounds that she was trespassing on matters beyond her authority. When Nala seemed hell-bent on squandering the treasury and ruining his people, Damayanti did not stay passive, saying that the rule of the country was none of her business. It is that gentle lady who entrusted the care of the young prince, the heir to the throne, with the minister, on seeing that her husband had taken leave of his better senses and judgement. Several such examples may be culled out further.

Human life is not something to be stored away under lock and key within one's house. Only when it becomes possible to claim that all human beings have nothing to do beyond their immediate dwelling-places, will it be possible to deny women admittance to affairs located beyond domestic boundaries. In the same way as the dwelling houses a small family, society itself constitutes a large family. It may be readily understood that problems will accumulate in a household where male or female members hold exclusive monopoly of domestic management. In Indian society too serious trouble has gathered because the intellect and the opinions of women have not shone forth brightly. Only that constant familiarity has numbed us to this reality.

It is hardly surprising that the prohibition on women entering public life has disfigured society. There will be significant physical and mental differences between men and women, as long as God's creation remains intact. God has created these two parties so that they may ensure each other's welfare and comfort. Qualities absent in the one are found in the other. God's will is that the virtues ensuing from these distinct temperaments and intellects must work for the good of the world in general. When we rule that women have no place in social and political affairs, we are transgressing God's decree. Compared to women, men have greater ability to identify the specific duties and tasks to be done in managing particular issues. However, Man has less of practical ability. Thinking and practical abilities are equally essential for the effectiveness of any endeavour. Similarly, the Womanly disposition possesses greater eye for detail and powers of judgement regarding the individual components or elements of any matter. This disposition would, however, find it difficult to grasp the matter in its totality. The Womanly temperament seems more suited to grasp the specific, and the Manly temperament is more inclined towards the general. Both are necessary in any situation, and one is as important as the other is. Thus, Womanly disposition exhibits several characteristics not found in Man. Woman is more prone towards minute observation of dealings in the external world. Man remains engrossed in his own thoughts and emotions. External goings-on would not catch much of his attention. Therefore, Woman has far more acute powers of observation.

In character too, substantial differences may be noticed. Woman's capacity for endurance is far greater. Man is braver, and more capable of courageous deeds. However, the stamina and grit to endure long stretches of suffering and disadvantage are lacking in men. This is one of the most admirable aspects of Womanly nature. Nature's dictates themselves illustrate this well. Each new birth is testimony to Woman's immense fortitude. She gifts each new life to the world, going as far as the banks of the *Vaitarani*[1] that separates the Living and the Dead. In the absence of the care she bestows upon it in its infancy, the new life would itself be lost to the world. It is no exaggeration to claim that the universe springs from the pain of Woman. Fairness and necessity both agree that Woman must be granted a role in deciding the future of the members of society—whom she brings forth in pain, nourishes and sustains.

Some argue that Woman ought not to concern herself with public affairs, as she has to bear the weight of motherhood. The reality, however, is the other way round. As long as God rules that maternity should remain exclusive to Woman, her intellect and opinions should be prominently reflected in all social matters. This is because Man will never know the value of human life with the intensity of Woman. Man may know far more than Woman about the economic conditions of society and its relations with other nations. Nevertheless, this knowledge alone will not bring advancement to any society, or to the world. An example will clarify this point. The people of nations all over the world have been keenly thinking of ways to prevent war. Yet the Goddess of Peace has not yet come as an incarnation into in this world. It is not difficult to see why. In the minds of male political leaders, disarmament stands contrary to their vested interests in conquest and expansion of trade. This underlies the reluctance in and disbelief towards demands for the reduction of warships. If women had the same eminence in social affairs as men, this situation would never have arisen. Woman can never rejoice at the sight of the earth being soaked by human blood even if it would bring about greater profits and wealth through trade. Woman cannot pass by the bullet-ridden corpse of an able-bodied human being with nonchalant and pitiless assurance. She will remember that each of those human beings was born through her own suffering. In the *Mahabharatam*, Dhritarashtra did not mourn the war.[2] It was the tears of blood shed by a woman,

Gandhari, which fell upon the lifeless bodies of the heroes at Kurukshetra.

This immense respect for human life apparent in the Womanly perspective surfaces not only in the matter of war. The destruction of human life in the world is not caused by war alone; sanitation, medical care, security for the needy, procurement of food for the people of the nation—all these raise or lower the average life-span of the members of society. If the sanitation arrangements of the city are not proper, the exertions of women to keep their homes neat and clean are all futile. If disease-causing foodstuffs are sold in the market place, then even if homemakers dedicate themselves wholly to the kitchen, food will not bring health. If there are not enough doctors to cure illnesses and midwives to attend to labour, then however affectionate and devoted mothers may be, infant deaths will never cease. How many die in the interior areas of India because enough midwives are not available at the time of labour? How many die because traders adulterate foodstuffs, like the milk necessary for infants? We are all familiar with such happenings. When it is pointed out that there are not enough doctors, hospitals and schools, today's rulers contend that it is impossible to allocate sufficient funds for such things because of the need for military expenditure. They consider the destruction of life to be more vital than its conservation. If women possessed as much authority in public life as men, such an opinion would surely not prevail in any country.

Besides medical care, women's minds ought to focus upon the fields of education, cottage industry and wage labour within the Nation. Today's education is flawed in that teachers are unaware of children's temper and are unable to share their thoughts, happiness and sorrows. The responsibility of maternity makes these qualities natural to Woman. An affectionate disposition should predominate in education. The system that forces some amount of information into the child, like bitter medicine administered with the stick, cannot be called education. Any education seeks to refine the mind and the character. Mathematics and other subjects, taught in schools are meant mainly to clarify the intelligence. If education does not invigorate the character and hone the ability to think and grasp ideas, then however much we may burden the brain, it will cease to be 'education'. To cultivate the intelligence, the qualities inherent in the child's mind must be fortified. This will happen only when the child is given essential warmth and freedom. However, along with this, the child's mind must not be allowed undesirable preoccupations. For this, the teacher must have the capacity for affection, the acumen to assess character, and other such positive virtues. It is Nature's law that any Woman must be her child's first teacher. Hence God has endowed women with the natural ability for teaching children. Irrespective of what the situation may be in higher education, the cooperation and opinions of women regarding basic education will prove beneficial.

Let us now consider wage labour and cottage industry. With Western innovation being increasingly accepted in India, machines and factories are becoming common. Though much is to be gained from this, a few evils also ensue. According to current arrangements, women are paid lower wages than men in all countries. Poverty is making it impossible for women to live as homemakers in the cities. Women are gaining plentiful employment in factories. The authorities are not adopting enough precautionary measures to prevent the breaches of morality that may occur when women work in factories in large numbers. Those who are learned in the science of the human body know well that heavy physical exertion near full-term pregnancy, and soon after parturition, is harmful to health. However, the rule that such women should be granted leave with full pay has not been yet fully implemented. A law to exempt such women from heavy labour would be insufficient; the responsibility of securing their lives must be borne by the employer. So also, the care of small children is being badly affected as their mothers are forced to go out to work. The factory owners must be made to bear the obligations of protecting and educating the children of their workers. If women had access to public affairs, all this would have caught their eye. Many laudable changes would have resulted. Such change has occurred in countries like England and America. It is worth stating that the attention of a few women's associations in India has now turned to this direction. The Women's Indian Association had worked for a resolution demanding compulsory education for boys and girls in the city of Madras. Their efforts have been successful. The Corporation of Madras has passed a resolution making basic education compulsory for boys and girls last March.

There are many other such matters that will benefit from the active collaboration of women, too detailed to be described here. One may also consider the objections raised to the participation of women in public life. The first argument is that the active involvement of women in public issues will deflect them away from motherhood and wifehood. Secondly, it is averred that even when women with vigorous public lives take up these roles, they will not be fulfilled fittingly. At first sight, these objections appear quite valid. However, some thought will reveal their pettiness. All women born in a society do not become wives or mothers. Some become widows. Some remain unmarried. The survival of society does not require that all women occupy such positions. We are not living in an uncivilized age. In those times, it was necessary to increase human numbers by all means. However, in the twentieth century, it is the quality of the population that is the yardstick of social advancement, not the strength of numbers. Is it not true that four crores of Englishmen hold in thrall thirty crores of Indians in their fist? Fewer numbers of healthy and intelligent citizens are preferable to large numbers of weak and ignorant ones. The idea that women in general may develop an abhorrence of motherhood is also misplaced. This is because the desire for motherhood is naturally inscribed in them. A few may forcibly suppress that desire. However, it is foolish to surmise that all women will behave so, or that they may succeed in suppressing their natural inclinations. Besides, women do have plenty of leisure after housework. Today that time is wasted in gossip and trivial conversation. Only good will arise through spending this time in public concerns and social service. Moreover, with middle age, motherhood itself ceases. Sons and daughters will be old enough to handle domestic duties. If women enter public affairs at that age, the training of children in life will also improve.

We must not deride these suggestions because they seem all Western. It is essential that we imbibe positive lessons from all. They are not contrary to Indian ideals in any way. The biographies of heroic men and courageous women of a society will give us insight into its condition. If there exists the impression that the ideal of women's freedom is alien to India, which has been sanctified by the lives of women of ancient times like Maitreyi, Gargi, Draupadi, Kunti and Gandhari, it is produced by sheer blindness. In Sanskrit, *sahadharmacharini* ['partner in the performance of Dharma'] is the synonym of *bharya* [wife]. A woman who brings all the meanings implicit in that term to fruition in her life cannot remain inattentive to matters that compel the attention of men. In India, our ancestor, Manu, said centuries ago that 'wherever women are worshipped, the Gods rejoice'. It is, however, futile for us women to feign dignity, uttering this sentence. No one will worship the undeserving. For that precept to become meaningful, the women of India will have to wake from their long slumber and live in full awareness of being the citizens of India. Only then will our Nation reach that exalted position that it richly deserves.

From 'Samudayattil Streekalute Sthanam', *The Mahila*, 4, 7 (1924): 250–57.

Notes

1   Vaitarini is the mythical river that runs around *Yamalokam*, the abode of *Yama*, the God of Death in Hindu mythology.
2   Refers to the Great War in the *Mahabharatam*. Dhritarashtra was the father of the Kauravas, who were decimated completely by their cousins, who also suffered grievous losses,

13
Vatakkecharuvil P. K. Kalyani

Vatakkecharuvil P. K. Kalyani was presumably one of the few active female satyagrahis during the Vaikom Satyagraha. She is probably the Kalyani mentioned in the report sent by the Inspector of Police, Vaikom, to the District Superintendent of Police, Kottayam, on 24 October 1099 M.E. (mid-June 1924), in which he says that three Ezhava women from Mavelikkara—Lakshmi, Karathoo Kunju and Kalyani—have arrived as satyagrahis (625/102,Vaikom Satyagraha Files, vol. 3).

An Appeal to the Hindu Women of Kerala

The Satyagraha at Vaikom is indeed a struggle for one of the fundamental rights of human beings, the freedom of movement.[1] Much of the life-force of two or three hundred people has been expended in this cause here, in this short while. We, who have only heard of mighty self-sacrifice in the stories of mythical figures such as Jesus Christ and Prahladam,[2] now witness it at Vaikom. Here we see martyrs who repose their faith in truth and morality, give no thought to adversity, and sacrifice the whole of their vitality in the face of violence, needless obstinacy and terror. There is no doubt that our victory lies in the future.

Dear sisters, what is our duty at this juncture? Is not freedom of movement essential for all? Large sections of women suffer from the lack of this freedom; is it not the duty of others to remedy it? Our menfolk provide us with models worthy of emulation in this matter. Is it not our duty to uproot the laws and customs that debilitate the freedom of movement of human beings? Mahatmaji's faith tells that we must strive incessantly to fulfil our duties. 'Did not Bhama, the beloved of Krishna fight in battle, did not Subhadra drive the chariot, did not Victoria rule this world?'[3] This is not the time to lean onto such examples. In truth, women have extended very little help to the Vaikom Satyagraha. We have suffered no austerities for it. A helping hand, though a minor one, was offered by our esteemed sisters from Mayyanad.[4] Like in many other matters, their handfuls-of-rice [*pidiyari*] collection has been exemplary.[5] Among the volunteers here, there are more natives of Tamil Nadu compared to our own people. Mrs. Ramaswamy Naicker shows herself as enthusiastic as Mr. Naicker in this.[6] Her capacity for renunciation is indeed admirable, a model for all of us. No matter how biting the rain or the cold; she is always beside us in our endurance with infectious enthusiasm. Mrs. Channar, too, is practising impeccable self-denial.[7] She is presently unwell. We need fifteen people to conduct the Satyagraha each time at all the four gates of the temple. This must include both *avarna*s and *savarna*s.[8] No savarna woman has yet come forward to participate in the Satyagraha. Probably no one realizes how ignominious this is. Now we are observing the Satyagraha only at the western and the northern gates. If we are able to get together ten people, we can save our face by organizing a Satyagraha exclusively of women at all four sides. The higher the social status of the participants ready for self-sacrifice, the more effective will our action be. Therefore a sizeable number of persons of high social standing, earned through education or otherwise, must urgently come forward into the struggle.

Women are capable of bearing the entire financial burden of the Satyagraha. The Ezhava community has opened a Satyagraha canteen through the handfuls-of-rice campaign.

It was opened on the first of Karkatakam [July–August]. If a canteen is being run from the negligible amounts of grain collected by the Ezhava women, the other expenses may be readily met by the collective efforts of other Hindu women. The residents of Mayyanad send us a tidy sum by their handfuls-of-rice collections alone. With some active effort, we will be able to accomplish a worthy deed easily, even if we limit ourselves to the natives of Travancore [Tiruvitamkoor]. How Mahatmaji would rejoice, if he heard that the Hindu Women of Kerala were piloting the Vaikom Satyagraha with their 'handfuls' of grain. Therefore I exhort you to make intelligent use of this opportunity to work for a glorious cause, this chance to beget the purpose of life. I invite the attention of all sisters to this issue.[9]

From 'Keraleeya Hindu Streekalodu Oru Abhyarthana', *Malayala Manorama* 24 July 1924.

Notes

1 The Vaikom Satyagraha (1924–25) was one of the important events in the anti-caste struggle in Kerala, specifically focused upon the issue of *teendal*, or distance pollution. The 'unapproachability' was such that the lower castes were required to keep a certain distance from caste Hindus. The Ezhavas, for instance, had to keep a distance of at least 16 feet, and the Pulayas, a distance of 72 feet. The latter had to proclaim their approach by loud shouts, lest their approach was not noticed by the upper castes. In Vaikom, the site of a major shrine to Lord Siva in Tiruvitamkoor, as in many other temples, the avarna Hindus were not permitted to use the roads running around the temple, while they were open to non-Hindus. For more detailed accounts, see Menon 1972: 116–35; Ravindran 1975. A brief account of women's participation in the Vaikom Satyagraha may be found in Velayudhan 1999: 493–95.
2 Prahladan, in the story of the Narasimha avatar of Vishnu, was the son of the oppressive asura king Hiranyakashipu, a sworn enemy of the Gods. Prahladan, however, harboured an unmatched devotion to Vishnu. He clung to his devotion despite the many trials he was subject to by his own father, refusing to chant Hiranyakashipu's name instead of Vishnu's.

AN APPEAL TO THE HINDU WOMEN OF KERALA | 89

3   The reference is to a shloka composed by Tottaikkattu Ikkavu Amma (1864–1915), in her much acclaimed play, *Subhadrarjunam* (1891), much quoted in such writings as these.
4   A village near Kollam in south Kerala, the native place of well-known Ezhava reformers and public figures like C. V. Kunhuraman and C. Kesavan.
5   Women's magazines like the *Sahodari*, (1 Jan 1925: 30), which were published by women active in Ezhava reformism made such appeals for *pidiyari* funds. Other pidiyari collections were being conducted by women for the Satyagraha elsewhere in Tiruvitamkoor. For example, T. N. Kalyanikutty Amma, who was to be well known in the nationalist movement later, initiated one such fund in Alappuzha (*Who's Who of Freedom Fighters in Kerala,* 1975: 190). The pidiyari collection seems to have a specifically women's way of raising funds for collective needs in Kerala earlier. For instance, among the Syrian Christians, in the late nineteenth century, the first Vicar Apostolic of the Vicariat of Changanashery, Mar Charles Lavigne, recommended that funds raised through pidiyari collection from homes must be devoted for nunneries with girls' schools attached to them (see Perumthottam, ed. 1999: 91).
6   The wife of the social reformer and campaigner against Brahminism in Tamil Nadu, E.V. Ramasamy Naicker, known as Periyar (lit. The great one). The author spells the name as 'Ramaswamy', but the reformer's preference because of his anti-Brahmin stance was for 'Ramasamy'.
7   Most probably the wife of a member of the wealthy Ezhava family, Alummootil. According to family sources, she must have been Mrs. Govinda Das, who was active in the Satyagraha. Indeed, the Channar's obligation to observe unapproachability around temples illustrated well the stranglehold of caste restrictions. Alummootil Channar was one of the richest men in Tiruvitamkoor in the late nineteenth century, and the owner of one of the few motorcars in Tiruvitamkoor. His driver was a Muslim. On approaching the temple roads, however, the Channar was obliged to dismount and walk a longer route, while his driver could drive through the temple roads, and would wait for the Channar at a certain distance.
8   Avarnas are outside the caste system and thus in the context of early twentieth-century Kerala, refer to the erstwhile untouchables including castes like the Ezhavas and the others who prefer to be known as dalits today; savarnas are castes within the caste system, above the so-called untouchables and arranged in a hierarchy of high and low.
9   The practice of issuing separate exhortations addressed exclusively to women was to become a regular feature of political and social activism in Kerala in the later decades. See, for instance, the appeal to women by T. C. Kochukutty Amma during the Civil Disobedience *(Matrubhumi,*

18 March 1930); appeal by K. Gomaty, Kayamkulam, 'Streekalum Nivarttanavum' during the Abstention movement in Tiruvitamkoor (*Malayala Manorama*, 20 April 1933); appeal by K. R. Narayani Amma against the *Murajapam* ceremony, which involved lavish hospitality to Brahmins at Thiruvananthapuram at the expense of the Tiruvitamkoor state, 'Streekalodorapeksha' (*Malayala Manorama*, 11 November 1929); appeal by Ratnamayi Devi in favour of the Temple Entry Proclamation, 'Kshetrapreveshanattinu Etirabhiprayamulla Sanatanikalodu' (To the *Sanatanis* who Disapprove of the Temple Entry Proclamation), *The Mahila* 17, 3 (1937): 90–99.

14

Konniyoor K. Meenakshi Amma

Konniyoor K. Meenakshi Amma (1901–80) was born at Konniyoor, in a well-known Nair family as the eldest daughter of P. S. Velu Pillai and Kutti Amma. She was the first woman from the district to have secured a postgraduate degree. She had a long and distinguished teaching career in Thiruvananthapuram, from 1925 to 1956. She was inspired by Mahatma Gandhi during his visit to Tiruvitamkoor in 1925 to become a well-known social worker in Tiruvitamkoor, a calling she took up with renewed zest after her retirement from service in 1956. She returned to her native village of Konniyoor that year, and became very active as a grass-root development activist, and played a very important role in bringing electricity to her village, in bringing modern health-care and family planning services to the region, in connecting the village to other areas by building a bridge across the Achenkovil River, and so on. She was honoured by her students and the local people in 1975 with a library built in the village named after her. She wrote extensively in magazines in the 1920s and 1930s, and was a respected public speaker. Her publications include Neenda Nizhal, Pushpakam *and* Atmabali, *and many other translations from English.*

Nair Women and the Home

For women, the Home is a sacred place; it occupies an important place in their lives. They are the unrivalled Empresses of that small Empire. Women alone can rule the whole world with quintessential ability while remaining located within the home.[1] The entire prosperity of a home rests upon the womenfolk. Without the constant attention and support of women, no home will improve. The community is but an aggregate of homes. Given this, it is no exaggeration to claim that the responsibility of rescuing the Nair community, which is facing a period of tumultuous change, from dangerous pitfalls, and reorienting it towards the blessed domain of prosperity lies with its women.

Considering the physical and mental makeup of women and their natural talent for homemaking, it may be readily understood that Goddess Nature herself has shaped them to be Potentates of the Home. However, the system of education prevalent today and the current trends in social reform attract women from the borders of the Home to various public domains. The dangers this may hasten in time for the community and, thereby, for the country are not negligible. It seems as though the Nair women who now flit about the skies of reformism harbour certain contempt for the Home. This is not at all desirable. The future of a community in which women perform their domestic tasks efficiently and hygienically is promising indeed. Christian succession assures that every Christian woman on reaching maturity is forced to take up the position of the mistress of a separate household. Therefore, she perseveres diligently from childhood in domestic work, and is thus well equipped to further the well-being of the home. She also passes on that enthusiasm and attentiveness to her man. This generates prosperity in the home, and the community advances.

With the Partition Bill, Nair women too have somewhat reached this position.[2] Once partition is complete, each woman will be freed from her [joint] family of origin and the guardianship of the karanavar and is compelled to establish herself by the strength of self-reliance. In this juncture we have no other way but to train our attention upon home management even more intently. The wound that the new Nair Bill has inflicted upon the community and the individual has to be healed through the powerful balm of efficient home management. Only good-natured and modest women can persuade their husbands to turn away from unnecessary expenses and practices and to lead them on to the path of advancement. The responsibility of ensuring that the property that may devolve onto oneself via partition is not squandered away or usurped by others falls heavily on the shoulders of women.

In home management, women should concentrate on helping men to rebuild the community, the economic foundations of which have fallen to pathetic depths. Some allege that Nair women are lacking in frugality and order. And this is more or less true. We must speedily remedy this defect. It can hardly be concealed that now Nair women who have gained a modicum of sophistication revile housework as beneath their dignity. Therefore in most Nair homes which are fairly prosperous, cooks are indispensable. Most people think that the greater the number of cooks, the more grand the display of breeding. As far as the officialdom is concerned, it is the easiest thing to see that this applies perfectly, word to word. What a sorry situation! Besides the wasteful expenditure incurred on account of these superfluous cooks, the women in the house gradually turn vain and lazy. The troubles and the losses they cause will be inestimable. Therefore, women should ensure that these 'inexorcizable ghosts' must be kept out of the home, as far as possible. In this matter, Nair women must emulate their Brahmin sisters. When conditions conducive to the efficient and hygienic performance of domestic duties have shaped up for us, why depend on others?

Once the housework is done, the rest of the day must not be spent in gossip; it must be devoted to the generation of wealth through productive crafts. It is essential that we be always engaged in some kind of work, however light, like the women of China. In this way, if we concentrate on economic affairs constantly, our mind will turn moral and upright, and consequently, God's radiance will fill our minds naturally. Lucrative trades like sewing, lace-making, poultry farming, and so on, may be begun. Why not enter into crafts like spinning, weaving, mat-making, coir-making and husk-beating? Each woman must necessarily own a charkha. That way, we will be able to take relief that we are performing our political duty too. Women are well placed to engage in animal husbandry and small farming. The expenses of the household can be met with the income from such occupations, without relying upon the income of the menfolk, and the rest can be saved. If many women can join in a rice chit-fund by contributing handfuls of rice, that will prove to be a good source of income. Money is an unavoidable instrument for success in modern life. Without money, nothing will be achieved in the world. The Nairs, who were once wealthy, have now become mostly indigent. That is the peculiarity of our mode of succession. But the arrival of the present mode of succession, which is conducive to the progress of the community, and is ordained by Nature, makes it possible for us to hope for a rosy future.[3] Only then will the lost grandeur of the Nairs be restored. Needless to repeat, all Nair women and men must toil together consistently towards this end.[4]

Though attending to the needs of the husband, caring for and training children and other such holy tasks fall within Womanly Duty, they will not be discussed here separately, as the focus of this article has been on the obligation to help the community economically through efficient home management. The women, who are the Goddesses of Wealth, must clear the way towards the uplift of the community. No greater fortune can bless the community if each Nair woman would take note of this and perform her domestic duty accordingly.

From 'Nair Streekalum Grihavum', *The Mahila*, 6, 4 (April 1924): 125–27.

Notes

1   The term used was 'Grhachakravarttinikal', which to my knowledge was first used by Chattambi Swamikal, a prominent spiritual figure of the early twentieth century, who was much-adored by many reformist

Nairs. It was frequently used by Nair reformers to highlight the invisible authority of the domestic woman. It was brilliantly contested in Travancore by Anna Chandy in 1929. See Essay 19, this volume.

2   This refers to the Travancore Nair Regulation Amendment (Regulation II of 1925), being debated in the Travancore Shree Mulam Popular Assembly and outside in 1924, which made significant changes to the Nair Regulation of 1912. It abolished polygamy; allowed partition of the joint family after the lifetime of the female ascendant, the eldest female member, and made women entitled to maintenance from their husbands.

3   This optimism was widely shared in these times. Yet the reasons for partition of particular taravads were quite distinct, and the process of separation was by no means painless. For an evocative portrayal of how individualization, the coming of new family values, which claimed to be 'Nature-ordained' and economic difficulties, made disputes and bickering present in the taravad for a long time, an excuse for its partition, see S. Menon Marath's novel *The Wound of Spring* (1960), set in the 1930s, in a taravad at the verge of collapse.

4   One may find exactly the same exhortation made to women of the other communities in these years. See, for example, speeches at the Shree Narayana Dharma Paripalana Yogam Annual Conference, 1928 (reported in the *Malayala Manorama,* 20 Feb 1928); speeches at the Araya Stree Samajam at Karunagappally, 1929 (reported in the *Malayala Manorama,* 6 May 1929); M. Lakshmikutty Amma, *'Nambutiri Balikamarute Vidyabhyasam'* (The Education of Nambutiri Girls), *Unny Nambutiri* 9, 1 (1927): 74–79.

15

Tottaikkattu Madhavi Amma

Tottaikkattu Madhavi Amma (1888–1968) was born in Ernakulam. Her mother, Tottikkattu Ikkavu Amma, was a well-known playwright whose play Subhadrarjunam *won much critical acclaim in the late nineteenth century.[1] Madhavi Amma gained proficiency in Malayalam, Sanskrit, English and other European languages and was known as a poet and critic. Her major works are* Hemapanjaram *(a translation of Sita Chatterjee's* A Cage of Gold*),* Saradamani *and* Tatvachinta. *She was active in the Ernakulam Women's Association and was nominated an unofficial member to the Cochin (Kochi) Legislative Council in 1925. She was the president of the Women's Conference held as part of the Nair Conference at Karuvatta in 1929. In 1932, she married the prominent Nair reformer, Mannath Padmanabhan. This short article was a response to a pen-portrait published by the* Malayala Manorama *in a series on the members of the Cochin Legislative Council.*

A Reply

I read the *Malayala Manorama* of the thirteenth Chingam (August–September). Let me greet you, first of all, for making my visage look attractive as part of your 'character sketches' of the members of the Legislative Council of Cochin [Kochi]. However, since I do hold that the work of newspapers, which perform the duty of popular representation in another fashion, is to circulate truthful news among people, inquire into their needs and point to solutions, I can, unfortunately, look upon that figure only as an instance of hyperbole.

I hereby, however, fulfil my responsibility as a member of the Legislative Council by making a clarification regarding your assertion that 'the vote in favour of the government during the debate about the Excise Department was probably out of the conviction that men are worse affected by the evils of alcoholism'. I do not have much to say, really. Women are not in favour of measures that bring harm to men. Moreover, I am aware of the fact that all women are not widows or unwed; and that even such women are unavoidably dependent on men in diverse ways. I would like you to know that since the mothers, sisters and wives of drunkards suffer deeply from such habits of their men, I would be the first to support prohibition on behalf of these unfortunate women.

In an issue which both the government and the people agree to be necessary for public well-being, but in which differences in policy choices—mostly hanging within guesswork—persist, I do not think that legislators should vote without explicit agreement, or for the simple purpose of showing off one's partiality to the people. Voting along with the government committed to the welfare of the people should not be read as a sign of being on the opposite side in intention. The issue just mentioned was one such. Therefore my humble insistence is that voting was uncalled for. It was an adjournment motion brought up to point out to the government that a 'difference in policy' was necessary to effectuate prohibition, put forward in the criticism of the Budget. A representative of the people also produced the contrary opinion. Therefore, it must be known, first, that both these opinions surfaced from the side of the people.

Now I have a few words on 'difference in policy'. The formulators of this argument have demanded that liquor shops should be closed down, and that trees must not be given for toddy tapping. Since there is no need to repeat here what the opponents of this demand had to say, I will cite only the government's policy. The government does recognize the evils of drinking; its interest is certainly to discourage it. For this, its policy has been to raise the taxes on liquor and gradually reduce the number of trees allowed for tapping. Other than this, if the guidelines suggested by the above members are to become acceptable in the small state of Kochi, the neighbouring [Tiruvitamkoor] and British Malabar should also consent to the same policy: shutting down the liquor shops and disallowing trees for toddy tapping. This was what the government had announced. Besides the urgency of generating consciousness among the people regarding the dangers of drinking, and seeking the most expeditious means towards this end has not been lost on the government. The easy and effective means identified towards this end was to institute sermons and other sorts of advice from the pulpits of churches, so as to reach the Christian population, which (as the formulator of the argument himself informed) is worst affected by the excesses of drinking. Here my objection was to the government's negligence in implementing an appropriate scheme of education that would direct individuals to honest livelihoods, making them aware of not only the dangers of drink but also all other social evils, from childhood onwards. I do believe that I have voiced this criticism before the government from within my own perspective, during the debate on the Education Department.

From 'Oru Marupadi', *Malayala Manorama,* 19 Sept. 1925.

Note

1 See Essay 13 n 3.

16
Mrs. I. C. Chacko

Mrs. I. C. Chacko (1892–1966) was born Nidheerikkal Mariam in a distinguished Syrian Christian family in Alappuzha, as the daughter of a well-known lawyer, Nidheerikkal Cyriac. She was educated in Thiruvananthapuram, passing the F.A examination from the Maharajah's College for Women However, unlike two of her younger sisters Teresa Nidhiry and Anna Nidhiry, who both had careers in education, she did not pursue her studies. At seventeen, she was married off to I. C. Chacko, who was to be known as a brilliant scholar and intellectual in Travancore. She was known to be an outspoken and uncompromising champion of women's rights. The article below is the speech she made at the women's meeting held as part of the All-Kerala Catholic Conference at Pala in Travancore 1924). I. C. Chacko's biographer notes that the speech created a veritable storm within the community, and that she and her husband received threatening letters after that (Ulakamtara 1995: 112). She is also said to have published a volume of stories titled Sanmargakathakal.

Our Women

Respected Ladies,

Several important events have occurred after our last conference. One of these is the birth of a princess in the Travancore [Tiruvitamkoor] royal family, under the star of Karthika. For the people of Travancore, who have in former times worried over the paucity of ladies in the royal house,[1] the fact that it is now adorned by three ladies, including the Senior Maharani, the Junior Maharani and the newly-born Princess, is one that gives much gratification. I congratulate the people of Travancore, and pray that the little Princess and the other members of the royal family be blessed with long life, health and prosperity.

Another event that has attracted our attention is that a decision has been taken to set up a statue of V. K. Parukutty Amma, the wife of the Maharaja of Cochin [Kochi] who has done much for the well-being of women and for public activities, on behalf of the public of Cochin. I hereby record our happiness, as women, about their decision, and express our willingness to extend cooperation.

The news that the governments of Madras and Cochin have nominated a woman each as unofficial members to their legislative bodies is, indeed, one that brings us great honour. I congratulate these two governments, but also express regret at the impropriety of the Travancore government in its not appointing a woman among the non-official members, despite the fact that it is ahead of these two states in women's education. I do believe that at least in the next election, this will be remedied.

I heartily congratulate all the young women of our community who have earned university degrees after our last conference. Among them, Margaret Paulose, who has passed the Literature Honours examination with very high marks, and won three university medals, deserves special mention. These young women have become our trailblazers, our guiding lights. We may justly hope that our womenfolk will steadily march ahead with these young women, and others like them, who have gained higher education. Anyway, the fact that women's education is spreading, albeit slowly, in our midst, is a sign of its promising future; the progress or regress of a community depends upon its women. There is no doubt that citizens raised by educated and cultured women will become refined, responsible and moral subjects.

Our Education

Many seem to be of the opinion that the education that we gain from schools and colleges today is inappropriate for women, and that they need to be trained in sewing, cooking, and so on. However, I do not agree with this view. Women who are constrained to spend all their time in the home with little children and ignorant servants definitely need higher education. Only through higher education are we able to interact with brilliant and learned scholars who were admired by the world in different times. It is through the knowledge in the sciences, literature and history that we obtain from the universities that we are enabled to connect our lives with those of the people of the past. We must remember that the ultimate goal of education is the widening of the intellect and the refining of character. This, surely, is necessary for everyone. Men, who ought to be more alert in the matter of wealth-creation, may probably require more of education to suit their professions. Besides, because they are engaged in activities that need them to get out of the home and travel far, they are more likely to attain refinement through close interaction with great personalities and seers, even without higher education. For women, the only way to acquire knowledge is through books. It is also improper to close down that path. It will be advantageous to train married women in taking care of children, nursing, cooking, sewing, and so on, after higher education, in the same way men are trained in professions of their choice like the law, engineering and medicine after passing the Intermediate examination or securing a B.A.

Our Marriage

Through Christianity has been established in India for many centuries, the customs and practices of marriage among us are seen to be not at all different from our neighbours, the Hindus. Since their religion permits polygamy, the Hindus insist that their girls are married of in their childhood [here the editor has inserted a clarification: 'among the Hindus of Kerala, child marriage is not insisted upon; nor is it the usual practice']. But I do consider it a great misdeed that we, who value life as nuns over matrimony, should display total negligence about marriage and related matters, and marry off girls aged twelve or fourteen. Where there is a law that stipulates that persons who have not reached the age of eighteen must not be permitted to alienate a property, parents who induce their twelve- and fourteen-year-old children to alienate themselves surely deserve punishment. This early marriage will always prove a blemish upon the sense of morality of these young women and men. No one thinks of the deleterious effects of child marriage. Married at an age at which they ought to be amassing strength of the body and intellect through games and study, these young girls are denied a chance to fortify themselves. Pregnancy and childbirth at a tender age foists unbearable burdens on them, and they soon become stunted and wane in health. Doctors are of the opinion that women ought to bear children only after their bodies have attained full maturity and vigour. Otherwise, childbirth becomes a threat to both mother and child. Human beings do not become fully mature before the age of twenty-five. Therefore the marriage of women before the age of twenty-four is inadvisable.

Our Infants

The health of infants depends upon the health of their parents. Compared to England and Wales, in India, a far higher number of infants die before they reach the age of five. Among the rest, three-fourths turn sickly in their infancy itself, and spend the rest of their lives as burdens to everyone else. Child marriage is one important reason why this happens. How will healthy infants be born to mothers who have not gained their full strength! The second reason for high infant deaths is the parents' ignorance of the proper way to raise children. A Baby Week is being celebrated once a year all over India as a means of alleviating this. In this period, expert doctors try to enlighten parents through speeches, leaflets, and so on. But uneducated parents do not cooperate with this. They continue to raise their children in the old established ways. A third reason for high deaths among infants is the poverty of the Indian people. One solution to this is women and men who do not have the capacity to support at least six children should refrain from marrying. To be born healthy, to have healthy food, to be educated well, these three are the birthrights of all infants. To defend these rights, under Indian conditions, the government must regulate marriage. I recently read in the papers that in a rule has been framed in Germany, by which everyone who gets married should necessarily obtain a license. We, who are scrupulous in our adherence to entrenched practices, too need to have such a rule.

Dowry

After the debate on dowry, it has become a topic of concern for everyone. As long as dowry stays in the woman's hands and she uses it freely, any degree of increase in dowry will only be salutary. In England, it was customary for the father of a woman, or her husband, or her husband's father, or all of them together, to put together some wealth in her name, because her progeny depended on her in their childhood, and because she could not go out and enter a profession, like men, and earn money. There is no one more concerned about the welfare of children than their own mother. She is forever and fully ready to spend all her money and time for their well-being. Besides, it is indeed a great relief to perceive, in children's affairs, that the mother and her wealth will be at hand, even if some mishap befalls the father and his wealth. However, the dowry system among us is a great shame. Though usually referred to as *stridhanam* [woman's wealth], it is, in actuality, *purushadhanam* [man's wealth]. In the same manner as a person buys a bullock or a horse for a sum of money, a father purchases a bridegroom for his daughter, paying a higher or lower sum commensurate to his qualifications. Our stridhanam is that price. That money is used up by the bridegroom's father as if it were his own, and the woman does not even catch a glimpse of it. This system cannot be deplored enough. The remedy to this, I feel, is the one suggested by Mr. Anthappayi, scholar and lover of the community, that the names of such parents who live by selling off their sons, and men who demand bribes from their brides' fathers in the name of stridhanam, should be published in the newspapers, and all social contact with them should be suspended.[2] As far as a woman's wealth is concerned, daughters must be granted a share equal to that of the sons as a right. Yet, in the Christian Right of Inheritance Bill of Travancore, Syrian Christian women do not have the right to inherit more than 5000 rupees from their parents' wealth.[3] I condemn the government that has passed this Bill that affects women's wealth too without knowing their inclination. I do believe that you will permit me to express here, as women, our protest against this Bill, and proclaim our desire that at least in women's wealth, equal shares must be assigned to both female and male descendents. The absence of landed property among Syrian Christian women of Travancore is a handicap in their attainment of voting rights to the Legislative Council and Praja Sabha, and this leaves them bereft of all rights in matters of ruling the land.

Women and Independence

Though slavery has been abolished for a long time in India, as far as Indian women are concerned, they are still slaves. They remain under the tutelage of the father in childhood, husband in youth, and the son in old age. Everyone ought to stay under the father's protection in his or her childhood. However, it does not seem that any woman will desire to carry on like a mere animal in submission to her husband, with whom she is on equal ground, and her sons, whom she brought up. Our indigence is the chief reason why our slavery persists. Pregnancy and bringing up children will not permit a married woman to take up a profession and make wealth, like men. As a solution to this, the women of England have begun to demand a right over a share of husbands' earnings for wives. We must agitate to put pressure on our government to make a similar law.

Firstly, we must embark upon home-based industries like spinning, weaving, making ornaments of gold and silver, painting, sewing, and so on, and improve our financial condition. Secondly, even if the incomes from these trades are negligible, they are sufficient to rouse our enthusiasm for work. There is the old adage that many drops make an ocean; everyone will be happy to find a livelihood by self-means. Thirdly, our ancestral wealth—that is, stridhanam—must remain in our own hands. No woman must accept husbands bought with that wealth. In this way, our slavery will gradually fade away, and we will be respected by other women. The situation being such that married women need to have professions that generate income, the policy of the Travancore government to dismiss women employees when they get married on those grounds alone is most reproachable.[4]

Reading

Though most of our women are literate, they are not found to be using that skill in practical life. The English author and poet Dr. Johnson recommended that a human being must spend at least five hours in reading. The heavy load of domestic work, it seems, will not allow women to spend so much time in reading books. Nevertheless, we must devote at least one hour a day to reading the newspapers, magazines and other worthy books. Women should subscribe to at least one newspaper and follow it regularly. Our knowledge will increase only through reading.

Women and Gatherings

Another thing is that we must pay attention to visiting; all the women of a locality should visit and get to know each other. Though women are said to love talk, Indian women do lead extremely lonely lives. There is no doubt that women, who are confined the whole day long with children and ignorant and lowly paid servants, will love to get together with their peers. European women consider visiting one of their primary duties. In order to see that the visits do not disrupt domestic duties, the time and days of visiting in the week are fixed. In those hours, they ready themselves to accept visitors in their parlours in neat clothing. This habit of theirs is worth imitating. As the familiarity between people grows, so will their desire to get together. Besides this, women should organize a club for themselves in all places. These should not be like schools; all women of the community should be granted entrance. Girls' schools may be used as clubs at least for an hour each day. In the club, besides friendly interaction, many sorts of exercise and games may be organized to strengthen their bodies and delight their minds. A club also helps us to read good magazines, newspapers, and so on. Such an institution can be easily run by a group of educated women in a locality. In places where women would find it impossible to take independent initiative, this could be done at least with the help and under their supervision of local notables, respected vicars and others.

 A few words about clean air and exercise are due in connection with this. The lack of fresh air and exercise counts highly among the reasons for the ill health of women. A noted doctor has remarked that simple physical exertion cannot be equated with exercise. Exercise rejuvenates the mind besides exerting the body. And again, it must be performed in the open, in ample sunlight. Doctors consider walking to be a good form of exercise. Walking exercises all parts of the body, and does not need much effort. Therefore it is suits women perfectly. It is very healthy to walk at least for an hour everyday in the evening, taking in fresh air and enjoying the pleasant sights of Nature. Since women spend most of their time in inner quarters, they should spend some time in the open to take in fresh air. And besides, bedrooms must be spacious and airy. The windows must not be shut in winter. It is enough to wear warm clothes.

Clothes and Ornaments

When Mahatma Gandhi visited Malabar, he was all praise for the white-coloured, short saris and mundus of the women of Malabar.[5] As far as the Christian women of Malabar are concerned, they do not deserve any such praise. Their waistcloths are so long that they are difficult to wash; though of white colour, they are so dirty that they appear black. At least our everyday clothes must be short and light enough to be washed every day. It is very healthy to bathe every day and wear fresh garments. White clothes let in sunlight, which is very necessary for health, much better than clothes of other hues. Therefore it is not good for women, and especially children, to wear such clothes every day. Many seem to hold the opinion that it is unnecessary to wear expensive ornaments and fabric like brocade and silk. Compared to Western women, we spend only a trifling amount on clothes and jewellery. As long as everyone wears clothes and ornaments in a way that suits their pockets, no one will have reason to complain. Moreover, we must remember that in these times in which unemployment is growing, if we cease to use brocades and ornaments, the workers who live by manufacturing them will lose their livelihoods. It is not possible to say that we reject expensive clothes and ornaments at all. Being ornamental objects, they please the eye.[6]

From 'Nammude Streekal', *Vanitakusumam*, 1, 6, M.E. 1102 Karkatakam (July–August 1924–25): 193–99.

Notes

1 This anxiety is typically a matrilineal one, since the absence of women members in a matrilineal family means that it would be left without heirs. The royal family of Travancore overcame this through adoption.
2 C. Antappayi (1863–1950) was a known as an author who completed O. Chandu Menon's unfinished novel, *Sharada*, and also for other works like the play *Naluperil Oruttan*. He was active in the All-Kerala Catholic Congress and a noted anti-dowry campaigner.
3 The reference is to the Travancore Christian Succession Act of 1916. For a detailed account, see Kodoth 2002. Dowry was accepted to have become a major problem in Travancore by the 1940s, and an Anti-Dowry Bill was introduced in the Shree Mulam Popular Assembly in 1946. During the discussion, both opponents and supporters of dowry agreed that this was causing the number of single women to go up, which was not desirable. *Proceedings of the Shree Mulam Assembly* vol. 20, 1946: 165–99. By the 1940s, Catholic women were actively campaigning through their own women's organizations, as well as through others such as the All-India Women's Conference for an equal share in family property, for example, during the discussion of the Cochin Christian Succession Act, which granted one-third the share of a son to the daughter. See *Proceedings of the Cochin Legislative Council*, vol. 8, 22 November 1940: 407–08.
4 This was a topic of much debate in Travancore, in the legislative forums as well, in these years. Nursing trainees, for instance, were made to agree to remain unmarried for five years after training, and devote themselves to government service. This was often questioned in the legislature, but the government took very long to change. Report, *Malayala Manorama*, 10 August 1926. In 1951, the All-India Women's Conference was still appealing to the Travancore-Cochin government to repeal the rule. Report, *Malayala Manorama* 7 September 1951.
5 Gandhi remarked that the white clothes of the women of Malabar reminded him of Sita following her husband into exile, and reflecting their 'internal purity'. *'Malabarile Streekal'*, *Sahodari*, 1, 3 (1925): 101–02.

6   The meetings chaired by the author at the All-Kerala Catholic Conferences seem to have been quite turbulent affairs. At the women's meeting, attended by some 500 women at the Catholic Congress at Pala (1927), which she chaired, one of the speakers, A. T. Mary, who had spoken about the necessity to serve one's husband, and keep quiet at times, was sharply attacked, and it was claimed that was not at all necessary, and women's right to a secure life and home was asserted. Violence, it was pointed out, was not to be tolerated, and it was recommended that women who were beaten by drunken husbands seek legal redress. Report, *Malayala Manorama*, 7 May 1927.

17

K. Mary Thomas

No information is available about this author.

Women's Independence

All human beings are created equal irrespective of their sex. However, a large section of the men, who are convinced of this, seem reluctant to concede equality and freedom to women, out of their selfish interests. Everywhere in the world, we see men who look upon the progress made by women with envy and distrust. Nevertheless, this does not mean that all men are selfish, or envious of women's struggle for independence. Men who willingly toil for the liberation of women may be found in all countries. It will not be appropriate to wield the pen without remembering such great souls with gratitude.

It needs to be admitted that there are many differences between women and men. Such divergences, without a doubt, are shaped by the dissimilarity in occupation and way of life. Since Woman is fully engrossed in domestic affairs, she has neither the time nor the facility to attend to or intervene in matters outside the home. In contrast, Man faces no such impediment. Consequently, men enter the tournament of life without fear and come away with many sorts of trophies. Who dare say that this is impossible for women? Only that women do not have the unimpeded opportunity, or the need for it.

Still, we do know that a few women have become capable enough for any sort of activity.

Man views Woman as if she were a caged songbird. There are many who declare that Woman should engage herself solely with domestic tasks, and remain within the home to foster the happiness of the household and of the householder, just as a caged bird is expected to sing melodiously and enchant the master. I do not proceed to accuse them, for they make these opinions without knowing the minds of women. However educated a man may be, he does not become capable of knowing the mind of a woman. Only a woman is capable of knowing the actual state and the disposition of another woman's mind. Women can only smile at men who think that women are playthings to be used for their happiness and fortune. They will certainly grieve much at male ignorance.

Women do not demand the position of the caged bird. They ask for equality and freedom. If these two conditions are realized, the world will benefit and profit from women in far greater measure. The condition and direction of the world will be completely transformed. It will be evident that a new Age is well within our reach. Any vehicle needs two wheels. If just one wheel turns, the vehicle will not move a foot. The situation of the world is similar to this. Woman and Man are the two wheels of this massive vehicle that is the world. Only when they move together will the world progress. Today, men are trying to pull forward the vehicle of the world by themselves. No matter how vigorously Man may pull, that huge vehicle will not get very far. Let him call to his Other Half (*Ardhanagam*), the Woman. Let him request her help. And then we may see how rapidly the vehicle moves.

All that is possible for Man is also possible for Woman. Man has not been able to beat Woman in even a single thing. Even in war, Woman will shine. The last World War [World War I] unveiled the true nature of Woman's strength to the world.[1] With it, men have become unable to continue announcing the weakness of women, as they used to. If women struggle for progress at this moment, men will not be able to obstruct them, as they did earlier. I do hope that my sisters will not waste this golden opportunity. Let us go forward hand-in-hand. We alone must struggle for our rights and freedom. We need not fear men in our struggle for justice; that is redundant.[2]

From 'Streeswatantryam', *Vanitakusumam*, 1, 7, M.E. 1103 Chingam (Aug–Sept 1927): 250–51.

Notes

1 Indeed, the active role of Englishwomen during World War I was much discussed in women's journals in Malayalam in these years. See, for instance, M. Chellamma, *'Streekalum Yuddhavum'* (Women and War), *Lakshmibhayi*, 10, 8, M.E. 1090 Vrishchikam (Nov–Dec 1914): 333–41; Chalayil K. M. Panikkar, *'Streekalute Sthitiyum European Yuddhavum'* (The Condition of Women and the War in Europe), *Bhashasarada*, 1, 2, M.E. 1090 Edavam (May–Jun 1915): 2–8.

2 Mary Thomas' views were condemned as truly excessive in an indirect attack in an article titled *'Atirukavinha Swatantryam'* (Excessive Freedom), written by Mrs. Sosamma Mancha (*Vanitakusumam*, 1, 8, M.E. 1103, Kanni (Sept–Oct. 1927): 287, which argued that too much freedom would direct women away from the home, and make them wanton, and that women ought to try and become productive and disciplined homemakers.

18

Editorial

This editorial is taken from the Vanitakusumam, *which was published from Kottayam in 1927 and was edited by V. C. John, who also edited the newspaper* Pratidinam. *It is said to have had a subscription of more than 2000, the largest of all women's magazines in Malayalam at that time, though it proved to be quite short-lived (Raghavan 1985: 147).*

Will Not Women Awake?

The elections and nominations to the Shree Mulam Popular Assembly are over.[1] The government of Travancore has not been benevolent enough to appoint a single woman member. We would, however, blame women themselves for the government's present unwillingness to appoint at least one member from womenfolk, who constitute the majority of the country's population. The work of intrepid struggle and sound bargaining to secure legitimate rights is the responsibility of women themselves. Any complacency on their part, induced by the hope that the government, which has displayed its conservatism in all affairs, will concede their rights and authority in full recognition of justice, and the mood of the times, would be most foolish. In all the countries of the world, women have won their freedom and rights only through agitation. These struggles have made it evident that 'only the infant that cries will have milk'. Travancore is no different from other states. It seems that here too, women will not be able to obtain citizenship and political rights without considerable struggle. This is but an opinion shaped by close observation of the modern conditions. Many are probably under the impression that the political freedom of women has been secured with the appointment of a woman member—albeit an official one.² However, even such people will not hesitate to admit that this is erroneous. The right to serve the country is not a male monopoly. Women have the right and the freedom to engage in such service. The women of the West have attained this. The women of the East have begun to emulate their exertions, and to enjoy the fruits of their labour a little. Travancore occupies an exalted position in the matter of female education.³ The number of women with higher education is not at all negligible here.⁴ The land of Vanchi [another name for Travancore] is indeed blessed in that it is the mother of many efficient and sagacious daughters, who may take up not only social leadership, but also exert political supremacy. Therefore, it may be claimed that women who are both eligible and able to render public service and capable of entering the Popular Assembly, Corporation Councils and Panchayat institutions are certainly not rare here.

Suffice to say, however, that the government is not prepared to acknowledge this reality, and even if it does so, to take pertinent action in its light. Each community is advancing the weight of its numbers and demanding representation in government service and public bodies; the government has proved quite pliable to their demands. However it seems quite reluctant to accede to the same policy of representation when women advance their claims on similar arguments.⁵ In these circumstances, all we can say to the women of Travancore is this. You must not while away anymore time in idle slumber. Open your eyes to the realities of the world, ascertain your needs, recognize your rights, and move to secure them. Do not ever harbour the hope that others will plead on your behalf and help you claim your rightful share, even in your wildest dreams. No history book has recorded such an instance in the world. Therefore, awake, fight for political freedom. You will surely have the support and sympathy of progressive men. In the current Popular Assembly, you have been granted no place. If this experience is not to be repeated in the coming legislature, your efforts must begin now.

From 'Streekal Iniyum Unarukayille?' *Vanitakusumam* 1 (11) M.E, 1103 Dhanu (Dec–Jan 1927–28): 387–88.

Notes

1 In 1888, a Legislative Council had been established in Travancore with nominated members, both officials and non-officials, as a purely deliberative body. In 1904, the Shree Mulam Popular Assembly was inaugurated in addition as a House of People's Representatives. The right of franchise was extended to women in 1919. Women became eligible to sit in the House in 1922 (Menon 1919: 60, 63). By 1940, 31.21 percent of the voters were women, according to the *Travancore State Manual*, vol. 1 (1940) (Pillai 1996:44).

2 There was a woman member in the Travancore Legislative Council, in charge of the Medical Department, Dr. Mary Poonen Lukose. The *Madras Mail* had dubbed her appointment as Durbar Physician and Administrative Head of the Medical Department as '*Feminism in Travancore*' (*Malayala Manorama*, 4 Oct 1924). Tottaikkattu Madhavi Amma was nominated to the Cochin Legislative Council in February 1924. In June 1928, Elizabeth Kuruvila was nominated to the Shree Mulam Popular Assembly, and Gauri Pavitran, to the Cochin Legislative Council. In the reformed Shree Mulam Assembly of 1932, women and men were given equal rights in voting and Membership of the Council. Two women members were to be nominated by the government. However, women who actually dared to contest faced almost insurmountable obstacles: Anna Chandy, contesting in 1931, had to face mud-slinging of the worst sort, and when she lost the elections, the *Malayalarajyam* wrote an editorial, full of unadulterated sexism, against her allegation of unfair tactics in an editorial in the *Shreemati* (*Nazrani Deepika* 2 Jujy 1931: 5–6). In 1940, a women-member, T. Narayani Amma, successfully introduced and piloted legislation, the Travancore Child Restraint Act, for the first time in the history of the Shree Mulam Assembly. Besides, several Malayali women were also entering the District Boards of the Madras Presidency in the 1930s.

For instance, in 1934, C. Parvati Amma was a nominated member of the Ramnad District Board, and First Class Honorary Magistrate at Madurai; K. Thankamma Jacob was the first elected Lady Councillor of the Coimbatore Municipality the same year, and of course, Ammu Swaminathan, who was a councillor of the Madras Corporation in 1934–39, whose career is better known.

3   Female literacy in Travancore for 1931 was 13.9 percent compared to an all-India figure of 2.4 percent. By 1941, it had gone up to 36 percent, compared to the all-India figure of 6.9 percent (Jeffrey 1993:60).

4   In 1929, there were 238 female students in the colleges of Travancore, according to the *Travancore State Manual,* vol. 3, 1940 (Pillai 1996: 695). According to the *Unemployment Enquiry Committee Report of Travancore* (1928), there were about 450 women clearing the higher examinations making them eligible for employment every year in Travancore (*Malayala Manorama,* 6 July: 28).

5   Indeed, these were times in which such demands were being vociferously made. In 1928, a 'Travancore Lady Graduates' Association' was formed with the intention of ending the unemployment of women graduates (*Vanitakusumam* 1, 11, 1927–28: 349). In 1932, Anna Chandy was arguing for proportional reservation in government jobs for women, and demanding the status of a depressed community for them (*Nazrani Deepika* 9 Aug 1931). Women-members of legislatures and women's deputations were making frequent requests for fair representation of women in public bodies and service (for instance, Elizabeth Kuruvila reported in *Malayala Manorama* 26 April 1929; memorial by women of Kunnamkulam to the government of Cochin, *Malayala Manorama* 30 July 1925). Newspapers were often warm in their support for such developments (see Editorial, *'Niyamasabha Nomination'*, *Malayala Manorama,* 20 June 1928). A Women's Conference held in Thiruvananthapuram in 1936 made the same demands for job-reservation and representation (*M.N. Nair Masika,* 1, 2, 1936:122–26). Major opposition came from proponents of communal representation, who saw it as effacing caste inequality, considering it primary. See two articles written by the well-known rationalist and reformer Sahodaran K. Ayyappan in 1935, *'Malayalarajyam Kanda Suvarna Rekha',* and *'Shreematiyute Vadam',* Ayyappan, 1965:11, .18.

19

Anna Chandy

Anna Chandy (1905-1996) was one of the most articulate representatives of the 'first generation feminists' in Kerala, but she is now much better known for her remarkable career. Brought up in Thiruvananthapuram, she earned a post-graduate degree with distinction in 1926, and went on to become the first woman in Kerala to earn a degree in law. She joined the Bar in 1929 and soon earned fame as an eminent practitioner in criminal law, and as an ardent champion of women's rights, especially in the publication she founded and edited, Shrimati. *She was a member of the Shree Mulam Popular Assembly between 1932–34, and was appointed First Grade Munsif in 1937, the first Malayali woman to occupy the post. In 1948, she became District Judge and a High Court Judge in 1959. She also served as a member of the Law Commission after her retirement in 1967. Her autobiography was serialized in the* Malayala Manorama *in 1971, and published under the title* Atmakatha *in 1973 (Thrissur: Carmel Books).*

On Women's Freedom

In this case our major argument is that this accusation is completely unfounded and lacks in optimism.[1] It has been brought forward with the intention of undermining the government's favourable attitude towards women, evident recently, and is contrary to fairness and justice. We also object that the complaint is invalid. From the elaborate petition, it is clear that the plaintiff's immediate demand is to ban all efforts by women to gain employment on the grounds that they are a bunch of creatures created for the domestic pleasures of men, and that their lives outside the hallowed kitchen-temples will harm familial happiness. 'Women necessarily need education. Those who are qualified must be allowed to take up employment and the professions,' argues the plaintiff, contradicting himself. First of all, we would like to ask where all these reformers were when fee concessions were being granted to women for English education, which has indeed destroyed the Eastern ideal of a Seelavathi-like chastity. For, as described in the petition, these artless women had been, indeed, spending all their lives in the interior of homes like caged songbirds. Where were they, when women were appointed as teachers on a salary of a hundred rupees as soon as they earned a B.A. degree? The present-day unemployment of women and their mad rush after paid jobs are but a consequence of their entry into higher education. The [former] speaker [Velu Pillai] gauges that it may be proved without much debate that women are best suited to stay at home. He has also quoted from Sakuntala's essay to Sankaracharya's Vedanta to applaud Womanly Duty. If so, why were women students shoved, eyes shut, along a path of learning, entirely inimical to this Duty, so destructive of Eastern Ideals?

Women who work hard at Differential Calculus and Public Finance should not benefit from it in practical life, indeed! If the modern *Manu Samhita* decrees that women should remain kitchen-idols singing the songs of someone murdering Mallan Pillai,[2] and limiting themselves like fleas devoid of self-respect to spending the twenty-five rupees produced by the B.A. holder-Husband's sweat and toil, then why spend lakhs of rupees on a First-Grade College for Women, and many thousands on Western lady teachers? What knowledge do these colleges provide women which would help them to become ideal mothers and blessed wives? All teachers, including the [former] speaker are culpable here.[3] I cannot fathom even now why he has proceeded to don the mantle of a Cassandra to make dire prophesies of social revolution or communal conflagration on the basis of a mostly anachronistic contention, which anyway implies that the readily-perceptible ill effects had been ignored for selfish advantage, in the first place. English education has been prevalent in our land for one hundred years. Women could well have been restricted to their homes on the pretext that they have been exclusively fashioned for such life. We object that instead of implementing the above measure, silence was maintained over the past one hundred years, and therefore this grievance is rendered obsolete. Besides, all teachers, including the [former] speaker, have misled women in their act of granting them qualifications for employment, and to argue thus after such deception cannot be valid.

The [former] speaker has stated that the dictum 'Woman deserves no freedom' is more or less extinct and that the women of Kerala are not slavish, especially those of the matrilineal communities, who, he claims, are the 'Empresses of the Home'.[4] His own speech testifies aloud that this is not always the case. The first lines of the shloka lay down that Woman must be protected by her father in childhood, by the husband in youth and by the son in old age. The article titled *'Atyavashya Parishkaram'* that fills nearly twelve full columns of the largest of Malayalam newspapers, the *Malayalarajyam,* unwaveringly hammers in the point that Woman should stay at home, and if married, she should stay under the guardianship of her husband. If the Woman is to stay wholly under the husband's protection, then how can one claim that the pronouncement 'Woman deserves no freedom' has indeed become defunct? In truth, that dictum from the *Manusmriti* of ancient times has been blended into the *Manusmriti* of the Kaliyug.

How is one to claim that women in Kerala are not in bondage? Women in the numerous castes and communities in Kerala occupy distinctly different situations. Antharjanams who are confined to the inner quarters with bronze bangles, the cadjan-leaf umbrella and the servant girl; Muslim sisters who suffer eternal hell in purdah, ridiculed by their menfolk as the soulless herd lacking the Adam's apple; Brahmin girls trapped in wedlock at an age in which one plays at mud-pie making, to become widows at the doorstep of youth, and condemned to live on with shaved heads, heaping curses upon life; Christian women, forever accursed by the harshness of dowry—all these are slaves who live in Kerala. Let us now consider the condition of the Matrilineal Domestic Empresses. Those who have lived in matrilineal arrangements know well that matriliny is but a chance product of political circumstances or social upheaval, and that it is ludicrous to view it as the banner of women's independence. What freedom do these hapless sisters enjoy in the matter of matrimony? Is the [former] speaker arguing that there are no sisters who have had to kneel before the avarice of the uncle or the brother, to consent to an arranged union, and lead agonized existences under the peremptory order that 'yours is not to reason why, yours is to do and die'? These women who take pride in the fact that property is inherited only in the female line, what substantial liberty do they hold? What we usually see is the passive holding of property, signing upon the dotted line drawn by the uncle or the brother. In any case, since the loyal followers of the community have already deserted this descent, calling it archaic, there is nothing in matriliny to set it up as the Pillar of Pride of women's freedom.

My humble opinion is that Nair women do not possess essential freedom. Nevertheless, in case my opinion is adjudged worthless, we would like to examine as our witness none other than the famous community leader, Mannath Padmanabha Pillai.[5] Let him testify on oath whether women in matrilineal families have been able to participate freely in the necessary efforts to revive the community. Recently, I had the occasion to be briefly enlightened about the freedom of women of matrilineal families at a village meeting celebrating Gandhiji's birthday. I, who had readied to speak a few words to the womenfolk on the affectionate insistence of the organizers, could not spy a single female infant within that expansive hall. On inquiring about this, I was told that though allowed to attend temple festivals and so on, women were yet to be permitted to take part in public meetings. When the record of women's freedom remains thus, there is no meaning in designating them as 'Empresses of the Home' or 'Sanctified Goddesses'. If these Empresses who may report at temple festivals to be pushed and tugged around, are not free to attend public meetings which are free of such discomfort, what is the use of the royal title? The [former] speaker waxes eloquent over the veneration of women as deities, and points out that we adore not Father India but Mother India. My wish is that women should not be worshipped as Goddesses; they must be treated as mere mortal creatures. What does Man, who worships Woman as Goddess and then desecrates her in stealth do? He condemns her to tragic suffering and takes refuge in the mores of society, shaped entirely by men. If trapped within immoral practice, the Woman ends up in perpetual hell, while the Man is ensconced in the Abode of Holiness. That is the hitch in being adored as a Goddess.

Until the day in which an evenhanded standard is forged to assess both parties alike, this sort of Goddess-worship remains hollow and inane. Are not women excluded from representative bodies like the Municipality and the Popular Assembly in a way that is certainly inglorious even for the matrilineal women whom the [former] speaker depicts as free in all respects? Those who club women with lunatics, are they going to worship women as Goddesses?

The [former] speaker is also insistent that we must not import and plant the saplings of dissent from alien lands that will cause women and men to gang up against each other in a clamorous showdown, and that such factionalism would lead to the disruption of the home, and the destruction of the family. One cannot help suspecting that some great social revolt is close at hand. The [former] speaker's assertion is that the desire of women for paid employment destroys the domestic bliss that he so warmly acclaims. This can be seen only as a mere figment of imagination. I do not see who is rousing the war drums today, which were never heard in those days in which married women began to work as teachers and assistant inspectresses and in which married attendants and doctors entered government service.[6] One can hardly help being reminded of Don Quixote's joust with the windmills when one witnesses this utterly unreal social calamity conjured up in an imaginary world, and desperately fought off with instruments assembled from every possible source, ranging from Ravana's death to the passing of Cromwell.

In actuality, I do not think that any woman graduate who has recently entered government service is married. I am informed that the lady graduates who have been employed at the High Court and the Secretariat are unmarried.[7] In that case no one needs to harbour fears that were non-existent earlier. The [former] speaker has agreed that unmarried women should be given employment. This appears contradictory. Either women, deemed the Guardians of the home, Generous Hosts and Husbands' Darlings, remain in the interior of the house as Chief Secretaries of Kitchendom, with no woman sweating after a job. Or, if they will be permitted to secure employment, it is my opinion that an exotic law that may bring considerable adverse effects in the future is not needed. If married women are denied jobs, they will only aspire to employment even at the cost of throwing off matrimony some way or the other. The [former] speaker has discovered a minor law that the majority of women in our country have an intense desire to marry and become mothers. If so, one would have to suppress the desire for maternity violently as a basic condition for employment. What will be the state of a country in which all women in higher education remain virgins lifelong, and all women employees, marriage haters? If the sole heirs of families decide to accept virginhood for the sake of employment, will not those families face extermination?

My fear is that the abhorrence towards marriage required of the progeny of ancient families as part of their jobs will wreck these well-established structures, just as one shatters massive rocks by piercing them and igniting gunpowder in the crevices. This opinion [the former speaker's], which claims to have ensued from the immaculate love of the Nation, does it require women of high education, intelligence and skill to remain dull blossoms in the Garden of Life, bereft of redolence, all for the sake of employment? The [former] speaker, who praises children as the pleasing transformation of one's own flesh and blood, born with bright faces and delightfully lovable words, the supports of our old age, the golden pillars of everlasting prosperity of the Nation, does he claim that the children should not be born in the land to capable and intelligent women, merely because they are employed? My humble conviction is that such reformism should not prevail among men and women.

The exposition 'An Urgently-Needed Reform' argues in sum that married women should not be granted employment by the government, and that if women desire employment, they should shun marriage. Many arguments have been deployed to establish this indefinite bit of thought. Let us examine them, one by one.

1. One reason advanced is that the self-respecting man would not accept the income generated by Woman's travails. What a blatantly arrogant and discriminatory thought! As if self-respect were the preserve of men alone! Is this to say that Woman, who must be Man's partner in sorrow and joy, must stay confined to the kitchen as despicable vermin, content with devouring whatever the husband may eke out of his labours, sometimes in ill-health, or seething with distress at the unjust practices of his superiors? Both parties require

sufficient amounts of self-respect. In that case, no one will feel outraged.

2. Another argument in favour of this *Manusmriti* of the Kaliyug that decries the employment of married women is that when a working couple reunites at home after work in the evening, the encounter of fatigue with exhaustion will precipitate a most uncomfortable situation for both. Though the veracity of this argument cannot be examined here in detail, a few words are in order. In the example used by the [former] speaker, it is not clear whether the wife of the peshkar [head of revenue administration] became a doctor, or whether a lady doctor's husband became a peshkar. The husbands who permit their wives to work are probably those who compare their wives' income with theirs, and find the latter more attractive, and are not perturbed by that their wives are not around in the house to remove their slippers, wipe their sweat, and perform other such servile duties, when they return from work. Therefore this objection is simply childish.

Indeed, those officials who saunter down to the gambling club soon after work, indulge themselves in pleasures of various sorts, and finally reach home when the cock crows, must necessarily have lady doctors for wives. On the contrary, what would possibly go wrong if the husband and wife rejoin after work, share and debate their day, and behave like true partners? If the stink of whisky is presented as the scent of eucalyptus, an officer wife may not swallow the lie. She may not accept the husband's nightly adventures as essential part of his official commitments. When both enjoy economic independence, the other may not meekly suffer the violent quarrels and autocratic commands of one. Therefore the husband who agrees to his wife's employment must necessarily be virtuous, and open to welcoming his wife as a companion. Is this harmful to the happiness of the world?

A further objection made in the [former] speech is that if both husband and wife earn, too much wealth will accumulate in the same house like the merging of the streams of the Yamuna and the Ganga. Behold! What an effusion of egalitarianism! If this logic is applied to men's employment as well, will anyone argue that when the sole heir of millions competes with the ardent devotee of the Goddess of Poverty, the latter is more deserving? Are jobs granted now on that principle? The Ganga-Yamuna merger need be feared only when such a 'Bolshevik' current of opinion gains ground in the land. In reality, if the clerk-wife of a man earning ten rupees receives a salary of fifteen, the family income will only be twenty-five rupees. What dreadful accumulation of wealth does this hint at? I do feel that this is but a baseless argument.

Another protestation is that working wives will be unable to care for their children properly. Though at first glance this may appear to be a credible argument, careful reflection reveals that it does not justify women's exclusion from paid employment. The mother's presence in the upbringing of a child is unavoidable only for some time immediately after the child's birth. Once the child starts school, even Kitchen-Deities get their chance at mothering only at night. I do think both working and non-working mothers can devote enough attention to taking care of children. And I do suggest that even if it falls a little below the mark, it will actually work to the advantage of the Nation. We may assess the relative sturdiness and health of infants if we compare those infants raised in mansions upon soft downy mattresses and swathed in woolly garments, to the infants of a farmer couple who are left entirely to their own wits early in the day. If we had not been unnecessarily obsessed with how children are cared for, then Indians raised altogether at the breast of their mothers would not have become the slaves of a race brought up by servants. It may also be seen that even fifty of our kitchen-yoked children will not match up to the daring and the stamina of a single white child. Since the [former] speaker has ventured forth into the world of insects and animals, let me glance at the world of Nature. Many may have noticed the cow push away its calf after it has grown somewhat. What does this mean? 'The period of guardianship is over now, stand on your own feet, seek food for yourself': this is what the cow gives notice of. In the same way, if we concede that the parents' responsibility is limited to raising a child from helpless infancy to self-sufficiency, then our children will prove that they possess the capacity for self-reliance, and rid themselves of the fragility of nerves that causes them to die of heart failure when the telegram announcing the results of the B.A. exam arrives. Let the advocates of birth control themselves decide which of the following is more injurious to society: the cruelty of parents who act without any thought of the mother's health, the father's resources and the needs of the older child, or the minor ills to be suffered in entrusting the child to the care of the servants.[8] Or, what would be wrong if the parents engage in a bit of renunciation, in self-control, for the sake of employment? Therefore, the insistence that women should waste away within homes in the interest of looking after the children should be abandoned. Those who are endowed with an abundance of motherly love are in any case quite unlikely to turn to employment away from their children, under any circumstance.

In short, I think that no woman should be sent to work in disregard of her wishes, physical condition and abilities. I merely insist that no discrimination based on sex or marital status must be made among those who have the necessary qualifications and desire for employment. It is quite possible that some married women need employment. How heart-rending it would be, if a woman seeking work under the dire circumstances of having to bear the burden of caring for a bed-ridden husband, and helpless little children, is denied work on the grounds of her marital status? That should not happen. It must be established that all qualified women, irrespective of whether they are married or not, are be free to take up employment.

How many are the respectable women who support their families on self-earned incomes? Whose salary ensured the security of the family of that renowned Deshabhimani, who was exiled for his valiant struggle against injustice in Vanchi [Travancore]?[9] If women were denied work because of their marital status, would it have been possible for that Paragon of Chastity to support her family thus? Has matrimony brought any disqualification to Shrimati Muthulakshmi Reddi, the Deputy Speaker of the Legislative Assembly at Madras? What about Sarojini Naidu who has spread the radiance of national pride all over the West, whom the [former] speaker himself extols as Goddess, is she not married, and a mother? If she had been compelled to stay behind kitchen-bars, would it have been possible for her to scale political heights inaccessible even to the manly men of India? Certainly, worthy women of the world have not been restricted by their marriages, nor have they been bound to kitchens. It is impossible to stem this unimpeded flood of women's freedom with the Dams of Kitchenism. Are not the women members of the legislative assemblies of Travancore [Tiruvitamkoor] and Cochin [Kochi] married?[10] What scourge has overtaken the country because Shrimati Chinnamma[11] and Mrs. Lukose,[12] well known for admirable social service and prowess in the medical sciences respectively, have tied the knot? We are gathered here today to celebrate the birthday of the respected regent Maharani of Travancore.[13] Does not her exemplary life announce that women with children can perform both maternal and public roles with remarkable competence?

Therefore let no woman be incarcerated in the kitchen on account of her marital status, let the paths towards freedom of employment and wealth creation be opened up to all women irrespective of their marital status. Those who have the enterprise, favourable environment and the ability for employment will seek it. Others will act according to the degree of maternal affection they possess. Those husbands who think that their wives' employment will impair the family's well-being need not send them to work. Besides, the married female-employee has the definite advantage of help and male support, compared to her unmarried counterpart. If a lady teacher handling classes in a (junior) college is married to a professor teaching in the graduate class, will she not be aided by her husband in teaching? If the lady doctor is married to another doctor, will not her curative abilities be superior to those of a single lady doctor? In short, the wife will be sent to work only with the full approval of the husband. If such a couple live in mutual fidelity, what social revolution is to be feared? What communal antagonism is to be foreseen?

An additional difficulty with the wife's employment, it seems, lies in the possible abasement that may have to be faced by the Woman Graduate forced to pay her respects to her superior officer and his ignorant wife. We will overcome this, taking relief in the fact that women too share in the affront suffered by the man forced to respect and salute his female superior and her ignorant husband.

The [former] speaker is also afraid that if women are allowed into jobs, they may disgrace men by working as daffedars [head-peons]. As long as all men are not daffedars, all women will not be peons. Just as the members of the male race range from emperors to sweepers, there will be members of the female race ranging from empresses to sweepers. Will they be obstinate that all women should be empresses or government secretaries? Even if they do, will that work? Given things as they are, is it appropriate to aver that women should not be given jobs because one may have to see them in the form of daffedars, lugging around boxes? Women usually seek work to help or support the father, the husband or the brother. Such men, who are the woman's guardians, will not direct her towards disgraceful occupations. Even if they do, even if women consent to such a great sacrifice for the sake of their loved ones, what is wrong with that? Besides, when did this infamy provoked by the sight of female daffedars crop up? Indeed, a mind that was never outraged by the sorry sight of many thousands of women carrying loads of paddy to the Chalai market for their daily bread, returning oppressed, cowering at the dirty comments passed by some depraved men, how it has been inflamed by the box-carrying of the female daffedars of an imaginary world!

Now, a few words are in order about the habit of quoting shlokas from the Smritis and Shrutis. The malady of justifying all sorts of inanities with shlokas is an epidemic that has infected the sharp, smooth chaps and the Scholars of Unfathomed Wisdom in our midst. A citation from a Smriti is culled out in case one wants to show the illegitimacy of post-menarche marriage for girls. When *Atirudram* [a sacrifice performed to propitiate the God Rudra] seems unavoidable to appease the authorities, yet another reference to the Shruti. If an authority upholding the *varnashrama dharma* is urgently needed, that can be made up with the *Sankarasmriti*. Plenty of shloka pieces too, to hold up the denial of widow remarriage. There can only be any hope for India when a cure is found for this affliction. We allege that the simile produced by the author to justify his argument, which requires that married women must roost in kitchens, and the scrap of a shloka deployed to establish it, constitute a deliberate effort to insult women. The *Treta* and *Dwapara* Ages have passed. The shlokas of these Ages have also turned to dust. Hence the recitation of shlokas to defend orthodoxy must cease.

In short, it is by no means expedient to load the responsibility of domestic strife upon those women who seek employment in order to support their menfolk. The bane of the land is precisely the reform that sets up the married-unmarried distinction as the principle of discrimination. We plead that this pointless reform is uncalled for. Those who do not need paid work and those who have not the health for it need not bother about employment. The large-hearted women who combine in themselves the *Vishalyakarini* and the *Mritasanjeevani* [two among the four divine medications] will manage motherhood and government employment the best they can. However, they must be allowed to utilize their natural talents only for the general good. If it is acknowledged that Woman too is a self-respecting creature and that she too has a share in the burden of maintaining the family, if women and men can live together in mutual constancy and oneness of heart, advance legislation to prevent a catastrophic clash will be rendered redundant. Women who demand representation in Parliament, government service, and so on, do not hanker to enter the army, or fight the French War. Is this not an ideal expression of their sense of discretion and discrimination? As long this good sense, praised by the [former] speaker, stays intact, could it not be reckoned that women would not seek anything that would sully their Womanliness or bring disgrace to men, like joining the army, hunting out criminals, or raiding for illicit arrack? If a verbal agreement is insufficient, we are prepared to put up the necessary bail.

Surely, economic independence is the foundation stone of the tower of women's liberty. It is this independence that women seek when they aspire for employment. Folks who take pride, in place and out of place, in that women are free in all respects, fire off speeches aimed at denying them government employment and other means by which the paths to economic equality may be opened up. The very contradictoriness of this can only evoke mocking smiles. If anyone retains any suspicion regarding women's capacity for service, they need only to refer to the recent comment made by a man who was an unshakable misogynist for many years: George Bernard Shaw. It was indeed he who said that women have much greater stamina and hence, efficiency, than the men who idle away their time in tattle-telling. We do not wish to extend this statement further. Hence we pray that the Honourable President-Justice,[14] known for his legal erudition and cultured views, may reject this inessential

ON WOMEN'S FREEDOM | 131

plaint, and allow us at least the travel fare from Kottayam. Some of the defendants do fear an adverse judgement since the Honourable Justice has himself expressed certain opinions seemingly favourable to the plaintiff at a meeting in Manacaud. And in case the judgement happens to be adverse, we will console ourselves by remembering that even the Sarda Bill had its opponents.[15]

From 'Streeswatantrytte Patti', *Sahodaran,* Special Number, M.E 1929: 133–46.

Notes

1 This article was a speech the author made at the Vidyabhivardhini Sabha, Thiruvananthapuram, a critical response to another speech made by Sadasyatilakam T. K. Velu Pillai (1882–1950), who was an eminent intellectual, legislator and writer of Travancore, well known for his revision of the *Travancore State Manual* (his speech was published by the *Malayala Manorama* titled 'Oru Atyavashya Parishkaram' (An Urgently Needed Reform), 15 and 29 Nov 1929. Velu Pillai's speech against giving government employment to women is the 'Case' referred to here by the author. She treats it as a petition filed against 'women', whom she proposes to defend, as a trained lawyer, in public, in a meeting chaired by a High Court Judge. The debate between Anna Chandy and Velu Pillai continued for some time in the *Samadarshi.* There were women who sided with Pillai: see, for instance, an article by P. Shinnammalu Kovilamma, *'Streekalute Purogati'* (The Advancement of Women), *Malayala Masika,* 1, 9 and 10, M.E. 1106 Makaram- Kumbham (Feb 1931): 258–68; 294–99 respectively.

2 This refers to a common folksong sung in accompaniment to the *kaikottikkali,* a dance which used to be performed by women on festive-ritual occasions in Kerala.

3 Velu Pillai taught law at the Maharajah's Law College, Thiruvananthapuram.

4 This was a view that enjoyed a high degree of circulation in Nair reformism, appearing as early as Chattambi Swamikal's famous address to the Ernakulam Women's Association in the second decade of the twentieth century (Maheshwaran Nair, ed., 1995: 808–12), and continuing to persist in the 1950s, for instance, surfacing in KPCC President Kumbalattu Sanku Pillai's justification of the poor representation of women in the Congress candidate list in the elections

of 1952 in Travancore-Cochin State (see statements by Kumbalattu Sanku Pillai, *Nazrani Deepika*, 29 Oct; 19 Nov. 1951).

5 Mannath Padmanabha Pillai (1878–1970) was the most influential of all reformers among the Nairs. He was involved in reformist activity since 1914, and founded and established the Nair Service Society, emerging as its life force since 1916, and acting as its Secretary for 31 years. He was active in the Vaikom (1924) and the Guruvayur (1929) Satyagrahas against untouchability and prominent as the leader of the 'Savarna Jatha' during the Vaikom Satyagraha. He was married to Tottaikkattu Madhavi Amma, who was a well-known public figure in Cochin, and member of the Cochin Legislative Assembly. See note on author, Essay 15, this volume.

6 Objections to the appointment of married women as government employees, however, had a far-older history in Travancore, surfacing in the first decade of the twentieth century itself. K. Chinnamma (see Essay 5, this volume) is said to have petitioned the Dewan P. Rajagopalachari regarding the impropriety of denying jobs in the educational department to married women (Nair 1947). In other departments, for example, in the medical department, controversy over employment of married nurses continued for long. See K. P. Nilakanta Pillai, query to Dr. (Mrs) Poonen Lukose during question hour in the Shree Mulam Popular Assembly, reported in the *Malayala Manorama*, 28 August 1926.

7 Four lady graduates were appointed in Travancore in 1929, G. R. Thankamma to the Secretariat, P. Chellamma in the Revenue Department, V. Ammukkutty Amma and Miss Hepzeba in the High Court.

8 Indeed, in the All-India Women's Conference of 1936 held in Thiruvananthapuram, Anna Chandy's resolution asking the government to supply necessary information to those seeking contraceptive advice through municipalities and other institutions, was passed amidst great controversy, and considerable indignation was expressed over a 'Christian woman' bringing forward such a resolution. See report on the All-India Women's Conference, *Nazrani Deepika*, 3 Jan 1936. She was almost the only person to defend contraception on entirely feminist grounds raising precisely the issue of women's control over their bodies. See her article *'Daurbalyabodham'* (Sense of Inferiority), *Malayala Manorama*, Special Issue, 1935: 14–5.

9 B. Kalyani Amma (1880–1942) was the first Nair woman to obtain a B.A. in Travancore. She was the wife of the radical journalist of Travancore, Deshabhimani K. Ramakrishna Pillai, and when he was exiled from

Travancore, she followed him to Malabar, working there. Her memoir *Vyazhavattasmaranakal* was much acclaimed.
10 Mrs. Elizabeth Kuruvila was nominated to the Shree Mulam Popular Assembly in 1928, and Mrs. Gauri Pavitran to the Cochin Legislative Council in the same year.
11 See Essay 5, this volume.
12 Dr. Mary Poonen Lukose (1886–1976) was educated in Thiruvananthapuram in the Holy Angels' Covent and the Maharajah's College. She earned her B.A. degree in 1909, becoming the first Malayali woman to do so. She then studied medicine in London and Dublin, and in 1915, became the first Malayali medical graduate. She entered government service in 1917, and became the Durbar Physician and the Head of the Travancore Medical Department in 1924.
13 Setu Lekshmi Bai (1895–1985), Regent Maharani of Travancore until the accession of Shree Chitira Tirunal Balarama Varma in 1931.
14 The meeting was presided by *'Sahityapanchanan'* P. K. Narayana Pillai (1878–1938), very well-known in Kerala as a brilliant scholar, critic, lawyer and legislator. He was president of the first Literary Assembly (*Sahitya Parishat*) at Edappally in 1927, a judge of the Travancore High Court and a member of the Shree Mulam Popular Assembly throughout the 1930s. His response to Anna Chandy's speech,which was made extempore, at a meeting in which it did not figure on the agenda, is to be found in P. K. Parameshwaran Nair 1972: 404–05.
15 The Child Marriage Restraint Act of 1929, also known as the Sarda Bill, which sought to penalize child marriages and raise the age of marriage from 12 to 16.

20

Elamkuttil Narayanikutty Amma

Elamkuttil Narayanikutty Amma (d. 1980) was born in the first decade of the twentieth century at Kozhikode (Calicut) in north Kerala. Her father Edavalli Narayanan Nair, was a lawyer. She graduated from Queen Mary's College, Madras, and worked as a teacher in Kozhikode She attained fame as a brilliant teacher and was deeply involved in the opening of a 'Baby Centre' at Kozhikode which offered health care for poor children. She was also active in the All-India Women's Conference, along with others like T. M. Narayanikutty Kovilamma and G. Kamalamma. Later she rose to prominence in the national movement as a propagator of Khadar and Hindi, and closely associated with well-known nationalists like A. V. Kuttimalu Amma and Verkot Ammakutty Amma. She was also keenly interested in the stage, and appeared onstage in the dramatic production of O. Chandu Menon's pioneering novel, Indulekha *(1889). She was known to be an excellent organizer, and much of the credit for the 'Swadeshi Exhibitions' conducted at Kozhikode in the 1930s went to her. She withdrew from public life after independence.*

Women and Khadar

Welcome to the eagerly awaited *Malayala Masika*![1] I hereby express my heartfelt gratitude to the organizers for reckoning me among the conductors of its birth ceremony. Let the merciful Lord Balakrishna bless the magazine so that it becomes a model for other publications in fortune, virtue, health and longevity, and sheds light on the whole of Kerala like an everlasting lamp. I am very happy to be given a chance to send this infant periodical a message. Nevertheless, I had been asked to write about any topic with the exception of politics.² Today, in India, surely, there seems to be no topic that is not related to the Nation, or to politics. However, since ordinary women like clothes and ornaments best, I intend to say a few words about the former.

Everyone knows that these are times in which we are all are obliged to persevere for the advancement of Mother India, irrespective of our sex. The times in which we were required to speak of women's education or independence are almost gone. What is the duty of educated women today? By education one means not just English education, but instruction that prepares them well for their particular duty. They have a duty to the Nation, which is as, or more, important than their duty towards their home. Even if they may not be able to do much in politics or community-life under present circumstances, they are probably in a better position to serve the Motherland economically. Merely that they need to pay some keen attention to understand the sheer poverty, exigencies and losses that have been our lot. We must think why poverty has made its appearance in India today. Was India always in this plight? Never. Once upon a time, Indian muslin and silk fabrics were famous all around the world.

English merchants entered India for trade. The foundations of their prosperity were established in that burning ghat in which they had reduced the spinning wheel to ashes. English merchants uprooted the cottage industries of the Indians and usurped their peace and prosperity. Some of us may ask why we must all hasten to revive this extinct industry, as we have all been divided into separate jatis, pursuing distinct sorts of occupation: would it not be enough to limit the protest to those who have been trained as weavers for generations? The answer to this question would be that this move intends not only to replace all the foreign cloth with swadeshi fabrics (in a short time), but also to provide an antidote to the sheer laxity displayed by a whole people towards this excellent industry.

The foreigner's formidable capacity for violence can be fought and quelled only through the pacific power of the spinning wheel. From ancient times, the hands that spun have earned India's food and freedom. Our salvation, truly, lies in the spinning wheel.

We must also remember that the revival of the spinning wheel will provide work and livelihood for thousands of our brothers and sisters, besides aiding the overall improvement of India's economic status. Our poverty will not cease if we merely wear khadar. Many of us may be wearing it. However, the present duty of Indian women lies in providing the thread to weave khadar. Are you strong enough to remain passive, even on hearing Mother India's sorrowful lament, which asks: do you wish to serve the millionaire-foreigner, or make a livelihood for your indigent sister? If not, then console the Mother, wipe her tears with the khadar you have made yourself!

Looking at the figures of some eight years earlier, the total length of clothing bought in India was 404 crore [each crore is ten million] yards. The clothing that serves as dress materials comes to an average of 12 yards per person. If all 32 crores of the population is divided up into families of five members each, how easy will it be for each family to produce the clothing it requires! According to the above figures each family will need 60 yards of clothing a year. Even if thread is spun only 25 days a month, the time necessary for producing good thread, and cleaning the cotton will take only two and a half-hours. Therefore, is it not certain that if a small portion of the time we idle away were spent in this, there will be much to gain?

Another difficulty would be about obtaining the cotton. Thinking of it, we need only 60 percent of the cotton grown in our country to meet our needs. Some may say that cotton is not cultivated in Kerala? This could be easily made up with some effort. Already, jute cultivation has picked up in some parts of the land. Likewise, each family will be able to raise the cotton for their immediate need for clothing. Figures say that half an acre of land will yield 20 pounds of cotton. All this is certainly not difficult for us who are long used to cottage industries. It is quite easy in Kerala. Besides, it could be shown that this will bring much profit.

The 16 crore tons of cotton harvested in 1922 from 180 lakh [1 lakh is 100,000] acres of land was worth 91 crores of rupees. The cost of 50 yards being ₹23, annas 8, each family makes a net profit of ₹12, annas 8, subtracting ₹11 for weaving charges and agricultural expenses. Some may feel that this is a trivial sum. Nevertheless, in Kerala, with a population of 80 lakhs, subdivided into five, on an average, if each family makes a profit of ₹12, the total profit would be 200 lakh (2 crore) rupees. Do we have no reservations about throwing away this huge sum, to be picked up by outsiders? Are we so rich? Even if we are indeed rich and busy, how many of us carry on in dire difficulty, wandering about as good-for-nothings? Is it not our duty not to dissipate this human existence, to make it beneficial for our brethren and ourselves?

These days, we find nothing but fancy clothes all around. But do my honourable sisters realize that not one yard of this belongs to us? Are we not ashamed that Mother India, who gave away clothing to the whole world two centuries ago, is seeking the help of others to cover her nakedness today? The foreigners have done great injustice to the Mother. Let the spinning wheel, which is none other than the *srichakram* of the Preserver of the Universe come to her rescue.[3]

From 'Streekalum Khadarum', *Malayala Masika*, 1, 1, M.E, 1105 Medam (April–May 1929–30): 15–20.

Notes

1 The *Malayala Masika* was published by a Women's Association called the Kottakkal Manorama Stree Samajam, and began around 1930. It was

one of the first journals in Malabar; it was claimed, to be 'run by women for women'. See 'Swantam Karyam', *Malayala Masika* 1, 1 (April–May 1930) : 2.

2 The practice of excluding politics from the topics discussed in Malayalam women's magazines is as old as Malayalam women's magazines themselves. The first women's magazine in Malayalam, the *Keraleeya Suguna Bodhini* (1894), stated this plainly (quoted in Raghavan:141). The *Malayala Masika*, too, was uncompromising. Its preliminary statement said: 'This infant should not be allowed anywhere near the political conflagration of the present' (ibid.: 4). However, women did partake in militant ways in the nationalist movement and the workers' movements. See, Menon 1972; Velayudhan 1999.

3 Refers to the weapon wielded by Vishnu, the spiked wheel, known as the *sudarshanam*, supposedly forged by the master-builder Visvakarma from the excess energy of the Sun God. This in fact was a common way of representing the charkha in nationalist speech and writing in Malayalam, which became highly popular through the poetry of Vallathol Narayana Menon (1879–1958), in which it appears as the Tantric *srichakra* and the *sudarshanam*. See Chaitanya 1971: 238.3.

21

B. Bhageeraty Amma

B. Bhageeraty Amma (1890–1938) was one of the most vocal advocates of an active, informed and disciplined domestic role for women in early twentieth century Kerala. She was well known as the editor of The Mahila, *one of the longest-lived women's magazines of the period. She was known to be a powerful public speaker, and was one of the women considered for membership in the Shree Mulam Praja Sabha in 1927 (*Malayala Manorama, *23 June 1927). Her major work,* Stree *(1925) described in detail her vision of 'active' domesticity as opposed to the traditional passive wifely devotion and was dedicated to 'the womenfolk of Kerala'.* Vijnanaprakasham *was another work. The following article was a speech she made at the fifth annual meeting of the literary assembly, the Kerala Sahitya Parishat. Her presence at the Parishat meetings did make a difference: in the meeting at Ernakulam, she argued against the practice of holding a separate women's meeting, pointing out that it was tantamount to segregating women, and that the decision that women should not be made speakers in men's literary meetings was misguided (*The Mahila *12, 4 and 5 (1932): 58). Her essays on modern womanhood, which appeared in* The Mahila *were collected in a book,* Sahityaramam.

Women and Literature

Those who seek to examine in detail the state of the social, material and spiritual culture of a people should train their gaze upon their literature. The greater the heights occupied by vernacular literature, the higher will be the regard for the people to whom it belongs. We must remember that the respect for India in other lands came largely on accord of its literature. Once foreigners were enabled to enter the treasury of Indian literature, they began to praise India's ancient civilization. Not satisfied with the knowledge of the ancient past gleaned from books, the students of history have begun to excavate repositories of knowledge from beneath the ground, lost to us in Nature's boisterous play. The stone inscriptions and other such remnants thus excavated have become invaluable treasures. These monuments reveal with pride the greatness of ancient India.

Humanity is forever in turbulence. Change and progress come naturally to it. Society never stays the same; nor does it turn back. Like the Arabian steed, it is imbued with the enthusiasm to charge forward, and struggles to surge in that direction. The human race, intent upon progress, cannot help expressing its life-ideals and thoughts in words. These expressions are the stuff of literature. What stage is society in? What are its life-ideals? Literary inquiry provides the answers to these questions. Human beings produce literature, which thus marks the condition of society. The writer circulates moral messages in pleasing language. The evil-minded are counselled about goodness, and the excitable, about calmness. Wealth-creation is recommended to the impoverished, and the wealthy are advised charity. The sorrowful are soothed with consolation, and the ignorant are given knowledge. The idle are made active, and the cowardly are turned courageous. Needless to say more, history offers evidence to prove that the truly talented author is capable of controlling and leading the society and the Nation. The literature of a country, and its history are bound together in this manner. This hardly needs any debate.

In speaking of literature, one is reminded of the verse that says:

> '*Lord, you yourself load the beggar's bundle upon the shoulder of kings.*
> *Lord, you yourself raise a fellow to heights in but a few days*'.[1]

Here a poet paints two distinct pictures and attributes them to God. In the same way we may claim here that both the progress and the regress of society are equally attributable to literature. Great ideals and thoughts help to uplift a society, and these enter human hearts through literature to purify thoughts and emotions. It is indisputable that the lack of fresh air will slow down blood circulation in human bodies. In the same way, a society without literary wealth will lose its vitality. Any society that thrives in this world in beauty and happiness is blessed with a wonderful literature. Now, I seek to unveil another picture beside this beautiful image.

What purpose lies behind the creation of Woman? Such a question is bound to come up, doubtless. However, just as the life-ideals of Eastern and Western peoples differ, so do their ideals of Womanhood. The Westerners grant primary significance to the external form: the shape, the radiance, the gesture. There is little contemplation of abstract qualities without attention to form. The material manifestations and external properties are crucial for them. They do not see the divine element that is merged in the material. The dignified place of women, their spiritual superiority never figured in their ideals. The Easterners, however, imagined the *prana* or the Divine Essence to inhere in the physical body. Feminine power is exalted thus:

> *You are the Will*
> *That brings forth the Universe.*
> *You are the Energy*
> *That preserves the Universe.*
> *You are the Force*
> *That destroys the Universe.*
> *Emerge in triumph,*
> *O Embodiments of Power!*

Such narration of spiritual energy seems rare in Western literature. Indeed, Woman, the very embodiment of spiritual energy, does possess the natural ability to recognize the frailties of the masculine character.

Literature is the ambrosia of thought, that is, the more it is enjoyed, the sweeter it tastes. Literature seduces Man by constant companionship. Woman is endowed with the inner energy to influence Man and the Affairs of the World by her gentle conversation, which is passionate and persuasive. Woman covers Man's mind with sweetness, slowly and delightfully, as if to test it. Men of evil ways are reformed by the strength of untainted Womanly character. The gentle and sweet power of a chaste wife can revive a man's vim and vigour, when he is tired and sick at heart. In moments of peril that render a man inert, the knowledge of his wife's sustaining presence will rouse him to victory over all dangers. The invisible power of the Woman can alter the very destinies of Nations. The responsibility of guarding the purity and the morality of a society, and the shaping of its character lies with the Woman. The social progress of countries rests more or less upon the virtue of its women and the respect they enjoy. The survival of a society, its pride, the mutual trust between men, the sense of justice, we must remember that all these are dependent upon the position granted to women in that society. A society that constantly insults Woman, looks upon her with lascivious eyes, reduces her to but an instrument of bodily pleasure and play, will soon deteriorate. The Woman must be looked upon as a Divine Power that maintains and protects social order. When this status fades, the society will be reduced to degeneration. Any society that is on the ascendant may be seen to be offering women proper regard and respect. It is foolish to think that one-half of humanity was created to belittle the contribution of the other half, and remain in enmity with it. The truth is that the male and female races were created to remedy each other's deficiencies and enrich society through the blending of virtues. We will readily admit that Woman, who holds within herself the ambrosia of love, is capable of delighting the whole of society. These arguments are sufficient to highlight that both literature and women are indispensable to any society that is on the path of progress.

Next we may examine how these fit together. Literature builds images from words about the manifestations of nature and the principles of life. It is comprised as poetry in prose and in verse. Both Woman and poetry are naturally endowed with certain inherent powers. Illustrious devotees of Nature transform these powers into forms useful for the prosperity of society. First, *Kavita* [poetry] and *Vanita* [Woman] resemble each other in significant ways. Language itself is imagined as a woman. Both have the quality of sweetness; *Kavita* and *Vanita* both cannot be forced; both are enriched by *alankaram* (meaning both 'literary device' and 'ornamentation'); both are capable of enlivening leisure hours. Richness of meaning and sweetness of recitation are essential to both. We find *kakali* [indicating both the name of a metre as well as 'fine, musical tone'], *kalakanji* [again, the name of a metre, and also 'waist-chain'], *annanada* [meaning both 'the use of light and gentle verse' and a 'graceful gait'] in both poetry and Woman. *Lalitapadavinyasam* [means both 'simple and graceful arrangement of words' and also 'light footsteps'] endows both literature and Woman with beauty. *Sadvrttata* [meaning both 'well-versified' and 'goodness of character'], gentleness, mutual agreement of ideas—all these are needed by both poetry and Woman. But noise, disorder, bad character/verse, lack of skill and so on, are ill advised. Thus we see that there is considerable resemblance, in form and function, between literature and Woman. These, which give wonderful form to the exquisite music that flows forth from the veena of Goddess Saraswati, are they not the two beloved daughters of Goddess Nature? These two creations make the world chaste and splendid.

If this truth is adequately grasped, the importance granted to literature and women in society will certainly increase. Women are generally of a passionate nature. Woman's talent for language, genius and powers of close observation gives a peerless loveliness to the image of Nature mirrored in her heart, in the form of the literary creation. Women have a natural talent for literature and therefore they are more dexterous at mixing the melody of Nature in literature. Women's literary efforts are more capable of making an impact upon the human heart. The stories of women authors who thus serve humanity will be doubtless edifying. Historians of literature who turn their eyes towards the ancient past will certainly remember Indian Womanhood with pride. They were unrivalled in the world; no female race anywhere matched up to them. Behold! The *Navamandala* of the Rig Veda has been recorded as the philosophical vision of the *Vagdevi* [Goddess of Words]. Scholars agree that the Upanishadic Sutras are found in their nascent form in these songs. When we reach the epoch of the Buddha, we find that he has a female following, with scholars like Vassita, Padachara and Tunga among them, who however, wrote in Pali, which we have not been able to read. Near the sixteenth century after Christ, we hear of wonderful personages like Mukta Bai of Pandharpur, Mira Bai of Chitor and Leela Devi of Kashmir. Mukta Bai and Mira Bai were devotees of Krishna, and Leela Devi, a devotee of Siva. We also know that there were scholars not only among Hindu women but also among Muslim women, and that they wrote poetry in Persian. In the South, Ambai, Ramabhadramba and others were prominent among Dravidian poets. Honnamma, the Kannadiga poet, is worth remembering. She was an ardent champion of equality between the sexes—a suffragist of sort. She was known to have written polemical poetry, unable to tolerate the scorn of men.

Let us now move on to Kerala. It will not be inappropriate to briefly examine the history of *Kairali* [Malayalam], and its present status. It will not be far-fetched to infer that both Kairali and the womenfolk of Kerala have come up through the same stages of life. The condition of Malayali women may be the same as the condition of the Malayalam language. The transformation of the lives of Malayali women parallels the upheavals undergone by the Malayalam language. In the present, the institution of university examinations has raised the importance of both the Malayalam language, and Malayali women. In the olden times, both enjoyed considerable eminence. Then, as the wheel of time turned, both lost their prominence. We also see them emerging now from the fall. To make this clear, we may briefly examine the history of both.

Before Malayalam separated from its root language into a distinct entity, our language was known as *Malayam Tamizh*.[2] There are many great works in this language, for example, *Patittuppattu*, which relates the exploits of the rulers of Kerala. *Chilappatikaram*, which describes the performing arts of this age, is also from Kerala. Its author, Illango Adikal, was a ruler in the line of the Cheras and the younger brother of the hero of *Patittupattu*, King Chenguttuvan. There is also evidence to prove that these potentates and their subjects were matrilineal. The Cheraman prince of Ennaikkadu Cherumandalam published the collection *Ainkarunnuru*, which contains songs by five poets. The grammar *Vembamala* by Aiyyanilattanar, which was distinct from *Pandy Tamizh*, was already prevalent then. All these are the rightful legacy of Kairali. Is it not an injustice that all these have been usurped by the Tamils and integrated into their literary history? It is painful to watch our wealth being stolen by others. The *Sahitya Parishat*, which includes scholars of law and literature,[3] should decide whether our claims still hold even though they have been advanced rather late. These works are excellent testimony to the robustness of Kairali in those times. Though the ballads of Taccholi are not very old, their content appears quite ancient.[4] They narrate many stories of courageous mothers and heroic warriors in the times of the *Perumals*,[5] and earlier. There is plenty of proof to show that women of those days were truly educated. We are informed that there exist documents, which show that women were trained as fighters, and lent a hand in overthrowing the alien regime of the *Perumals* and earning independence for Kerala. How virtuous and refined their minds must have been! And how pathetic the present condition, a result of a great fall from these heights!

After the period of the Perumals, the contact with Tamils weakened. The nobles of Kerala who had initiated self-rule could not rule united, and were divided into small loci of power, within tiny principalities. *Malayam Tamizh* too cast off from *Pandy Tamizh*. The mutual strife of rulers destroyed the peace of the land. At this juncture, the language of Kerala, too, was orphaned. It was compelled to rely upon Sanskrit, the language of the Aryans. The very same calamity befell the women of Kerala. The internal strife of the rulers and the Mughal inroads destroyed the peace and prosperity of the country. Women, too, became dependent. The Brahmins bound the society of Kerala in the chains of religion. The women of Kerala were subjected to evil customs, and degraded to the condition of domestic animals. The Supreme Court verdict of *Na Stree Swatantryamarhati* [women deserve no freedom] was also pronounced. Even when Malayalam began to emerge as a distinct language, and gain in strength, the evil days of the Malayalis did not abate. Recently, however, this misfortune has begun to recede.

In this way, once the language of Kerala transformed itself into Malayalam, it was shaped into a separate language by the Great Poet Tunjan[6] and further nourished by the poets Cherussery[7] and Kunjan.[8] With the benevolence of the Education Committee and the political awakening, Malayalam can now match up to other local languages, and she now produces an abundance of offspring.

In these times, the status of Malayali women paralleled that of the language. Once the infighting between nobles ceased and unrest ended in the land, the women of Kerala were more able to express their natural talents. The condition of women in those times may well be inferred from the fact that the first Guru of Aroor Bhattatiri, the author of the *Uttaranaishadhakavyam*, was a woman, Manorama Tampuratti.[9] She was followed by several scholars like Umadevi Tampuratti of the Changanashery Palace, Kuttikkunhu Tangachi[10] Tottaikkattu Ikkavamma[11] and the Nagercoil Ammachi.[12] Many are presently engaged in literary pursuits.[13] We may also remember here our sisters from British India who are engaged in literary work in their mother tongues and other languages: Toru Dutt, Sarojini Naidu, Swarnakumari Devi, Sita and Shanta Chatterjee and others. Under the influence of modern education and revival in the political field, the women of Kerala have begun to reclaim their freedom, and the children of modern enlightenment are growing in numbers. Thus, examining the transformation of the language of Kerala and its women, we find that their histories have moved along almost the same path. Let the culmination of the agreement between literature and women turn out auspiciously, with the blessings of Goddess Kairali.[14]

Mothers who do not rejoice in an abundance of children and mothers who do not wish to see virtuousness in their children are rare. In the community's perspective, the strength of numbers is desirable, but in the race of life it causes frustration. The present is a moment in which Malayalam is giving birth to large numbers at a rapid rate. Political visionaries and popular representatives are issuing warnings to people that birth control is necessary even today, and that without birth control, scientific or non-scientific, the future holds terrible dangers. In the world of language too, birth control is being publicly announced. It is a declaration that brings both joy and sorrow to the mother. As the saying goes, 'the lack of strength in children is better than the perverted strength of children'. Scholars who find this entirely compatible with worldly wisdom have instituted scientific literary criticism as the means of birth control in literature. Insubstantial and ignoble works should not be permitted to enter the temple of literature. Doing so will hamper the growth of literature, the virtuous life of society and moral domestic existence. Some English scholars claim that criticism rears its head only when literature is in decline. But greatness cannot be attained without criticism. It is hoped that the attention of the lovers of the language will turn in this direction.

While expressing one's satisfaction at the advancement of Malayalam, one is also disappointed at the huge gap between the number of women who have acquired higher education, and the number of women who have turned to literary pursuits. It is regrettable that those who have gained distinction in their study of foreign literatures do not bother to achieve excellence in their own literature. The poverty of articles we now experience, in a situation in which the number of graduates is growing, is indescribable; the grief I express, having engaged for the past years in journalistic work, quite possibly, is a product of self-interest. Some time back, a few persons wrote to me that they were finding it difficult to write articles in their mother tongue. I had not the least doubt that they were telling the truth. I am happy to say that upon accepting my suggestion to read certain books at once, and give some special attention to the use of words, they have now become quite proficient in writing prose. Most authors are reluctant to try hard enough. That attitude is inimical to our own betterment. Women who desire political equality should not display a lack of will in literary endeavours. That is a breach of duty. I do regret having to state that the sisters who have gained higher education are no less guilty in this matter, and that this is certainly a shame. A change in this sorry state would be welcome, so that a bright future may be expected.

Before I end this speech, I would like to make one more point. The literature of Kerala must be urgently protected from contamination. It must grow without abandoning its national character. Like a particular society, a particular literature too has its unique features. It is said that a person's wealth of ideas lies in his veins. Human beings are scrupulous in protecting the purity of blood, and taking on an aristocratic bearing. Womankind is marked by a certain intensity: the fundamental principle of marriage is the preservation of the purity of blood, and the vitality of society. Marriage must effectively enhance the essential qualities of society, its radiance and energy. Marriage with aliens leads to the admixture of blood and the destruction of the ideas and and a way of life unique to a society. What will be the consequence of marriage between two completely different individuals whose social ideals are vastly apart? Bound together by love, they stay united for some time under its spell. As the blood cools, so does the attachment. Nearing old age, the memory of ancestors and the race reappears. Then, in this, second childhood, with increasing detachment to food and company, both parties recognize their errors, become hostile, and regret their decision. The last phase is swathed in gloom. There is reason to fear that in our eagerness to multiply the wealth of our language, we may make illegitimate liaisons with foreign ideas that do not suit our uniqueness, and in which the latter take the upper hand. In this case, the fate of the ill-matched couple just mentioned will befall the language. This is not to say that changes appropriate to moving times must be banned: change is the law of Nature. But we must remember even as we imitate the foreigners that they zealously preserve their traditional identity. Reform should not surpass necessity. Take in the better elements; why absorb the unnecessary? Reform is not meant to disrupt smooth and peaceful social life. Reform must be tailored to suit the unique circumstances of the Nation and the community. I would only plead that the deluge of reform should not sweep our identity down into the sea where it would sink without a trace. I would like to close my words by expressing the hope that the patriotic fervour and the enlightenment of women will prove useful in this matter.

From 'Streekalum Sahityavum', *The Mahila*, 11, 1 (1931): 16-26.

Notes

1 From the *Jnanappana*, written by Poontanam Nambutiri (1549–1640), a well-loved poet during the Bhakti movement.
2 This part is summarised from an article by Sri. K. Sankara Pillai B.A. (B. B. Amma).
3 Well-known lawyers and judges like P. K. Narayana Pillai and Malloor Govinda Pillai were active in the *Sahitya Parishat* meetings.
4 Folk ballads from North Kerala, which narrate the stories of warrior-heroes like Tachcholi Othenan.
5 The reference is to the *Keralolpatti*, a Brahmin-centric myth of origin of Kerala, which claims that Parashurama created Kerala raising it from the sea, and gave it away to Brahmins to atone his sin of having slaughtered Kshatriyas. The Brahmins settled here were unable to live in peace with each other. Parashurama instructed them to bring a king—a *Perumal*—once in every 12 years from an alien kingdom. Twenty-one such Perumals are said to have ruled Kerala, the last of whom is said to have converted to Islam and left for Mecca, dividing his kingdom among his lieutenants. Bhageeraty Amma, of course, sees the end of the Perumal rule as a result of deliverance from alien rule through struggle.
6 Tunjchattu Ramanujan Ezhuttachan, the author of the several *Kilippattu*s [a distinct genre of poetry that made ample use of classical Dravidian metres] in Malayalam, revered as a father figure, who lived in the sixteenth or seventeenth centuries, whose *Addhyatma Ramayanam*, *Mahabharatam, Bhagavatam, Harinamakirtanam* and *Devi Bhagavatam* are still read widely in Kerala. He is considered to be the best known representative of the Bhakti cult in Kerala.
7 A founder-figure of Malayalam, who lived in the fifteenth century, whose work *Krishnagatha* remains one of the best loved works in the language.
8. Kunjan Nambiar, the great Malayalam poet of the eighteenth century, whose works for *Tullal* performances (a form of verse narration with the accompaniment of music and dance movements with exuberant humour) drew upon Puranic themes, but critically portrayed eighteenth-century Malayali everyday life with considerable verve and humour.

9 Manorama Tampuratti (1760–1828) was of the *Samutiri* royal house of Kozhikode; well known for her scholarship, especially in Sanskrit grammar.
10 Original name, Lakshmikkutty Pillai (1820–1904); born in Thiruvananthapuram; 'Kuttikunhu Tangachi' was her pet name. Her major works are *Shreematiswayamvaram Attakatha, Thiruvananthapuram Sthalapuranam, Sethusnanam Pana* and *Ajnatavasam Natakam*. Some of her works have been collected in Guptan Nair, ed, 1979.
11 Tottaikkattu Ikkavamma (1864–1916), born in Kochi, poet and dramatist, whose *Subhadrarjunam* (1891) won much critical acclaim. Her other work was *Nalacharitam*.
12 Original name, Kalyanikutty, born at Mukundapuram near Thrissur (1839–1909); 'Nagercoil Ammachi' was her title as wife of Maharaja Ayiliam Tirunal of Travancore (Tiruvitamkoor). Her major works are *Rasakrida, Ambarishacharitam, Pativratya Panchakam*, and *Satya Panchakam*.
13 Indeed there were many Malayali women in the nineteenth century who were active in literary pursuits, both in Sanskrit and Malayalam, of whom the women of the royal houses are better known. A few examples are Rugmini Bai of Travancore (1808–1837), the sister of Maharaja Swati Tirunal; Lakshmi Bai Tampurati of Mavelikkara (1847–1900); Lakshmi Tampurati of Kadattanad (1844–1908); Ambadevi Tampurati of Kilimanoor (1832–1887); Ikkavamma Tampuran of Tripunitura (1844–1921); Ambadevi Tampurati of Chembrol (1890–1928).

By the 1930s, modern educated women were beginning to enter the field of modern literature as short story writers (for instance, N. Lalithambika Antharjanam 1909–1988); as poets (N. Balamani Amma 1909; Kadattanad Madhavi Amma 1909–1999; Mary John Tottam 1901–1985 ; Koottattukulam Mary John 1905–1998 ; Mutukulam Parvaty Amma 1904–1977), and translators as re-tellers of the Puranas. (T. C. Kalyani Amma (1879–1956); Taravattu Ammalu Amma (1863–1936). There were also many others who continued to produce works in the traditional literary modes, producing *shloka*s, *kavyam*s, and so on, for example, Mangalasherril Kochukunhi Amma (1854–1922) and Tekkekkunnatu Kalyani Amma (1896–1942).
14 The practice of language adoration was prevalent somewhat but it stayed at the level of language alone: the Tamils actually set up their language as the Goddess Tamizh; Kairali never got to be a Goddess.

22

Parvati Nenminimangalam

Parvati Nenminimangalam (d 1947) was born in Irinjalakkuda in Thrissur district. She became active in the Nambutiri (Malayala Brahmin) reformist work after her marriage, and soon rose to be one of the most outspoken and radical female voices within it. She was one of the chief organizers of Ghoshabahishkaranam (breach of seclusion) actions of the Antharjanams (Malayala Brahmin women), which were of vital importance in their challenge to traditional restrictions. She was also a key figure in the drafting of a petition by Antharjanams asking for a separate forum for Antharjanams at the Guruvayoor Conference (1931) of the radical wing of Nambutiri reformism, the Nambutiri Yuvajana Sangham. As a member of the Legislative Council of Cochin (Kochi), she was part of the Select Committee appointed to inquire about the opinions of the community to the proposed bill:. Cochin Nambutiri Bill (ultimately passed in 1932–33). In fact, a section of the Nambutiri orthodoxy petitioned the Maharaja of Cochin that they were unable to give evidence before the Committee as Parvati Nenminimangalam, a member, was an outcaste (Nazrani Deepika, 10 Jun. 1932). She was known to be a powerful, provocative public speaker. The Mahila described her in 1932 as the 'Joan of Arc of the Nambutiri empire' (The Mahila, 12, 3 and 4, 1932:159). Many of her articles appeared in the 1930s.[1]

Womanliness

Something put together for great poets to describe; a form shaped for men to feast their eyes upon—a hoax, plainly. But a beautiful assemblage that we adore—yes, Womanliness is a creature that worships bondage as matter of pride.

I ask, do we not today take pride in our servitude, in our craving for pompous show? Men must toil, earn money, get ornaments made, soft mattresses filled and velvet jackets stitched. And we should adorn ourselves with all this, carrying on placidly upon those mattresses. That is Man's desire, Woman's pride! If a woman labours in a field, she is dubbed vulgar! If a woman does not wear a velvet blouse, her neck is not covered with jewellery; she does not wear a saree with brocade – she falls below the mark! Where, then, are we to find freedom?

With the very same tongue that makes appeals for liberation, we nag our husbands for brocade sarees, gold ornaments and subjection! Do we not today take to such clothing styles and ornaments just to seduce men? God has already differentiated Woman and Man at birth. Why separate again with contrivances? Only to dupe each other.

Why should we grow our hair long? Simply to waste three hours a day at untangling and combing it so that it shines. Why swathe ourselves in so many garments like torches with many bits of cloth rolled around? Certainly not to cover the body. The arms of the blouse shouldn't be more than an inch long, nor should the neck be narrow. Even if two or three garments are worn, only half the body should be concealed. How ideal a mode of dressing!

Wearing a neckfull of ornaments serves merely to cause default in interest-payment, and fill the coffers of the jewel merchants. Ears and the nose are pierced only to be filled once more with diamond-encrusted pins. Continuing thus, how many are the lewd vanities we smugly submit to? Where is freedom for us unless all this is smashed?

Irrespective of whether this humbug was made the law by men, or fashioned by women on their own, it serves no other purpose but seduction. We do not need to seduce men; that is coarse and despicable. A woman must seduce only her husband. But not by fraudulent decking up. We will definitely have reason to regret if we marry men thus deceived by our guileful apparel. We may be sure that as soon as our adornments are soiled, they will retract. One must seduce only with genuine affection—Love. Such Love is within the power of any woman; that alone will suffice to seduce the husband.

If I have a word, we will attain freedom only through casting out the usual practice within which we remain frail. We should get rid of our fancy attire and adornments; it is necessary to cover the body, but it should not serve ostentatious display. Women and men need no difference in clothing.

Education is essential; but it is not necessary that one must study in a school. Women must acquire special training in home management and in looking after children. Work is not dishonour, but dignity. For both Woman and Man, earning one's own livelihood is certainly a matter of dignity. Women will gain their true freedom and Womanliness only when they toil alongside men, diligently and well.

From *'Streetvam', Stree,* 1, 1. M.E. 1108 Edavam (May–June 1933): 15–6.

Note

1 See also the note on her by Premji (M. P. Bhattatiripad): 'Parvati Nenminimangalam', *Unny Nambutiri,* 1, 2 (1947): 63–73.

23

Narikkatiri Devaki Antharjanam

Narikkatiri Devaki Antharjanam, popularly known as 'Devaki Narikkattiri' (1912–2000), was one of the most prominent of the Malayala Brahmin women who came into public life in Kerala in the 1930s, defying the strict traditional seclusion (ghosha) prescribed for Antharjanams (Malayala Brahmin women). Born at Koppam near Palakkad, she was brought up in an orthodox Malayala Brahmin household. Her husband, Vamanan Narikkattiri, was an ardent reformer. She was excommunicated from her family along with her pro-reform husband and his brother for their activism. Later, they opened an eating-house near the Brahmasvam Matam at Trichur (Thrissur) named 'Sudharnnavam'. Along with this, she continued to be very visible as a public speaker. She was attracted to political affairs, and was an inmate of the Wardha Ashram for some time. Later she drew close to Communist politics and worked at the Party's commune in Kozhikode. Several of her articles were published in the 1930s.[1]

Women Should Not Abandon the Kitchen

The struggle for women's independence has become intense in these times. Modern women are striving to gain equal rights and representation along with men in government jobs and legislative bodies. They have begun to intervene in issues that affect the whole world today. Thus to remark that women should not abandon the kitchen, when they are fighting for comprehensive freedoms, may sound narrow and unsophisticated to many. Besides, many may ready themselves to attack it with disdainful objections. I say to them: I am a woman. Yes, I am an Antharjanam [a Malayala Brahmin woman. Literally, 'a resident of the Inner-Quarters'] who has borne for some time the bitterness of bondage. I too wish that women should have freedom and responsibility, and that their service must secure the well-being of people. To achieve this, it is very necessary to retain one's hold on the kitchen. I will spell this out further. Though weak and fettered, we do have, to a certain extent, influence in the kitchen. If we deploy this power with a sense of responsibility, our bondage and weaknesses will depart hastily. Moreover, the kitchen may be regarded as an ideal site from which one may serve the world. Basing our efforts on the kitchen will go a long way to foster the reform of custom, health, moral consciousness, and other such matters.

Referring to the reform of custom can elucidate this fact. These are times in which the struggle to destroy untouchability is quickening. But protest is largely limited to conference halls and news features; it has not yet begun to set foot in the kitchen. This is a major shortcoming. Actually, today, the kitchen is the place where untouchability and other evil customs are entrenched. There are many today who leave the progressiveness and lofty ideals they profess in public outside their doorstep, not daring to bring them inside the home. Why is this so? Because women's efforts have been inadequate, I would say. It is the primary duty of the women to banish baneful customs from the kitchen and foster enlightened ideas there. Many egregious customs, ridden with superstition, are observed within homes. Women are usually responsible for this state of affairs. Generally, in all families, it is the opinion of the women that is reflected in internal affairs. If they try sincerely, it will be possible to instil enlightened ideals in homes within the space of a generation. Children are raised within the ambit of the mother's influence. The common practice we see is that of mothers imbuing their children with superstition and faith in outrageous customs, along with breast milk. In place of this, mothers ought to strive to inculcate in them such worthy qualities as courage, patience, truthfulness and the sense of independence.

Food is the major source of health. It is prepared, of course, in the kitchen. Cooking is not servile labour. On the contrary, it is a task of much consequence. It is our foremost duty to acquire practical proficiency in scientific ways of preparing food. Persuasion is the best way of ridding society of bad habits, like drinking, which are harmful to both body and mind. Thus society has much to profit from efforts focused on the kitchen. In sum, the kitchen is the engine of the ship that is the community. Women are its captains.

Esteemed readers, please do not misunderstand me: all that has been said does not mean that I am in favour of women limiting themselves to nooks and corners within kitchens, shut away from sunlight. Women must enter any high status deemed essential for humankind. They must be capable of doing any sort of work. Women must win full freedom to defend their sense of dignity and fulfil their commitments. One cannot but say that the kitchen is the foundation of the community and that women are chiefly responsible for how it is. From cottage to palace, everyone can partake in reforming the kitchen. Indeed, reform that does not root itself in the kitchen cannot be long-lived.

From 'Streekal Adukkala Upekshikkarutu', *Stree*, 1, 1, M.E. 1108, Edavam (May–June 1933): 24–25.

Note

1   For a first person account of Devaki Narikkatiri's life, see Anandi 2002.

24

Pennammabhayi, Chambakkulam

No information is available about the author. She seems to have hailed from Chambakkulam, in the Kuttanad region of Kerala, Alappuzha (Alleppey) District, as her signature indicates.

Our Economic Position and Women

Today the economic position of the people of Kerala does not appear laudable in the least. This critical situation is worsening day by day. With Western sophistication on the horizon, material necessities have swelled oppressively. The prices of essentials have been shooting up. According to economic theory, the value of money has been steeply falling all around the world. In order to live comfortably today, a family will require four to six times the amount of money that was necessary for a comfortable life fifty years ago. The times when men were contented with a mundu [waistcloth: a dhoti that hangs from the waist to the ground] and a neryatu [upper cloth to wear around one's shoulders] and a shirt at most, are long gone. Today one cannot be dignified without a mundu, a neryatu, a shirt, a collar, tie and footwear. Instead of the cadjan leaf umbrella that could be bought by exchanging three *idangazhis* [a Malayali measure] of paddy, today we see the Java 'Alpaca' umbrella. The needs of women have exceeded all this. Today the *pavada* [skirt] the jacket, the silk sari and bangles have attained unprecedented presence in Kerala.

Now we have diamond jewellery instead of gold ornaments, silk garments instead of *kasavu* [gold brocade]. If one is to recount all the increases in expenditure, the list will be endless.

It is high time we seek out ways to secure our economic position, which is now very vulnerable. This problem can be resolved only if women direct their attention towards the acquisition of wealth. It is really pathetic to see that a householder with a wife and six or eight children has to provide for this large family by himself. It is also quite regrettable that our women have no thought about this situation. We are under the impression that it is Man's duty to earn money for the needs of his family. What are our women up to after the husband has left for his hard labour after a meagre breakfast? They roam around the neighbouring houses, boasting and bragging; the rest of the time is their siesta. Beside, if the man's hard-earned income proves insufficient, a severe tongue-lashing will be his lot. If he dares to mention any of his troubles, pat will come the sharp retort that he 'ought to have anticipated all this'. No doubt, this situation must undergo a complete change.

Today we hear all around the clamour for women's freedom. This is certainly necessary. But no one considers whether our womenfolk have the capacity to be self-reliant in their lives. Men and women who have acquired even a modicum of sophistication are today clamouring for the entry of women into the legislative bodies, and so on. Yet they do not ponder whether women are capable of standing on their own feet or not. Today's womenfolk would not mind starving for three days, but would look upon getting out of the house and seeking a solution as a great blow to their dignity and gentility. I do not blame women for this state of affairs. Long centuries of slavery have made women lose all their vigour. If capacities remain unutilized over generations, they are sure to become extinct. Women's vitality has been lost. A false belief in the respectability of present inertness has also set in. So also the idea that Woman is weak. All this must be swept away in time. Society can never improve otherwise. Woman must enter into agriculture, trade and cottage industry. Failures and difficulties may be expected at first. They must be considered the heralds of future success. Men are somewhat less than half of the world's population. Today the world subsists on their labour. The remaining half is inert. Just think of the difference that will be made if both parties enter the field of labour. Because Woman stays within the home distant from labour, Man harbours towards her a certain emotion admixed with pity. What is the consequence of this? Men have decided unanimously that Woman is good for nothing. Woman has no right to rule the country; she has no say in the leadership of the family. Everything remains with Man. [But] once it is evident that Woman can perform any sort of work efficiently, this situation will change; or, it will have to be changed. Therefore it is argued that Woman too must enter the field of labour, instead of indulging in debate and making ineffectual exhortations.

The Sanskrit proverb about everything being dependent on gold is truth itself.[1] Let Woman prove herself adept at acquiring wealth, she will acquire both freedom and status. There is reason to raise a problem here: If Woman proceeds to engage in labour along with Man, who will manage the home? In reality, however, home-management does not require much time. It is not time-consuming work. Today it is assumed that the woman in the house, or all the women present there, are engaged in home-management. In truth, they are merely whiling away their time in the absence of other enterprise. Home management needs to be granted only the status of a sub-task to be performed in between other activities. What are the items counted as housework today? Snoozing along with the child on the pretext of putting it to sleep; going off to the neighbour's house on the excuse of borrowing something, to make potshots with missiles of envy and bluster; passing on whatever ill-treatment one has suffered at the hands of one's mother-in-law with compound interest to one's daughter-in-law, if she is present; nagging the servants; grumbling about one's terrible workload to one's husband to win his sympathy—these would be the major items. Kitchen work and other tasks are minor items. With some alertness, housework is not burdensome. That is why it is recommended here that all women should engage in various sorts of labour. It is not being argued that everyone should take to the farms and the factories, or set up shops. Each one must have work befitting the particular person's situation. The bad name that women are useless must go. What is wrong in a woman performing clerical tasks for her husband? Why cannot a woman be the house-manager for her farmer-husband? Why should an educated woman hire a tutor for her child? She should do this herself. If we cling on to false pride, our economic condition will deteriorate. All women must think about this subject and act appropriately.

From 'Nammute Sambattikanilayum Streekalum', *Vanitakusumam* 1, 9, M.E. 1109 Tulam (Oct–Nov 1933): 315–20.

Note

1   *Sarvegunah kanchanamashrayanti.*

25

Parvaty Ayyappan

Parvaty Ayyappan (1902–1998) was born in Kurkanchery in Trichur (Thrissur) as the daughter of Judge E. K. Ayyakkutty. She was educated at Queen Mary's College and Lady Wellington's College, Chennai (Madras), and later became a teacher at the Vivekodayam School, Trichur. She also worked in Sri Lanka as a teacher for a year and later at the Government Training School at Trichur. In 1930, she married the well-known rationalist and reformer, 'Sahodaran' K. Ayyappan, and they were active in reformist endeavours She brought out the women's magazine Stree *in 1933. During World War II, she worked in the Women's Auxiliary Corps. In 1956, she retired from government service to form the Sree Narayana Sevika Samajam, and the Sree Narayana Guru Alwaye Advaita Ashram at Aluva along with Ayyappan. She was active in public life until 1988.*

On Womanly Duty

I happened to see a lot of news about the life of Mussolini's wife in the papers recently.[1] She takes no role in public affairs. She spends her time fully preoccupied in the affairs of her own household, maintaining it to be her sole duty. This information is presented as though Mussolini's wife ought to serve as a model for women in general and homemakers in particular. It is possible that she lacks the talent to help Mussolini in his political and administrative work, or participate in other public matters. If that is so, then her decision to adopt a way of life that makes her useful within a manageable and circumscribed field is indeed laudable.

However, this need not be upheld as a model for women. The misconception that the capability and the duty of women lie mainly in wifely tasks and home management is what makes this way of life appear worthy of imitation. The capabilities and duties of women and men do not lie in their becoming good wives and husbands. Nature has nurtured in individuals certain instincts for the preservation of the race. Particular sorts of male-female relationships have been shaped through the stirrings of such instincts. The Husband-Wife relationship and modern domestic life are the cultured versions of these. Women and men have many duties to fulfil that go well beyond them. Women and men must labour alike for the progress of humanity. For this, the intellect, and other qualities intrinsic to both men and women must be developed. There is no male-female difference in this matter. Gender distinctions do not apply in humility or intelligence. It applies only to lower qualities. Since Nature has assigned Woman the duty of bringing forth offspring, women had to devote all their energy and attention to tasks like childbirth, taking care of children and domestic management. Consequently, unlike men, women were unable to express their mental and other abilities. Therefore, if women gain the time and the facilities to develop intellectual or other faculties with the adoption of birth control and other excellent inventions of modernity, they will be able to make a mark upon all the areas of life which men enter and secure success in.

If that is to become reality, then the foolish notion that the home and the kitchen are the sites of Womanly Duty must be obliterated from the minds of people. Indeed, if women who have the capacity to emulate the wifehood of Marie Curie, whose partnership in Pierre Curie's scientific research caused the world to be blessed with Radium, imitate Mussolini's wife, society and the world would stand to lose. Those women of ancient India, who engaged Yajnavalkya in debate, they too would not be like Madame Mussolini. How marvellous is the example of Nadezhda Krupskaya, who accompanied Lenin all through his trials and difficulties, through the periods of his incarceration and exile, experiencing destitution and the rigours of underground life, serving as a secretary in his heavy labours. India would have lost a great social worker if Pandit Jawaharlal's wife had contented herself with the management of Anand Bhavan. Ideal marriages are those in which husbands and wives cooperate in each other's duties as far as possible. Such a relationship ought to be upheld as an ideal model for the people.

From 'Streedharmatte Patti', *Shrimati* Annual Number 1938: 44.

Note

1 Such articles were quite frequent in the late 1920s and 1930s: see, for instance, 'Streedharmam', *Deepam*, 1, 4, M.E.1106, Vrischikam (Nov–Dec 1930): 126; 'Mussoliniyute Patni' in 'Vanitalokam', *The Mahila*, 17, 3 (1937): 99–100; V. C. Kuruvila, 'Mussoliniyute Patni', *Vanitakusumam*, 1, 12 (1027–28): 444–48. Indeed, this was an important topic debated in the 1930s, and not only in magazines. The students of the Maharajah's College for Women, Thiruvananthapuram, for instance, were debating on the motion 'Hitler's exhortation to women to stay in the interiors of homes is unfit for modern times' in 1939. See *The Women's College Magazine* 2 (June 1940): 70–1. The motion was carried.

26

Ittichiriyamma

There is no information about this author.

Womenfolk and Reform: Matters Necessary and Unnecessary

I do not think any of you will like my name. You would all be quite gratified if it were some neither-male-nor-female name like 'Sarada Madhavan' or 'Kalyani Krishnan'.[1] In fact, you would be satisfied if my name were 'Ittichhiri Krishnan'. However, I am not inclined to renouncing my femininity and becoming sexless.

You may remind me of the 'Radhakrishnan' of yore. Well, there is nothing to be surprised if a man with sixteen thousand and eight wives falls into femininity. And not just that. You have to remember that 'Radhakrishnan' was Krishna's name; it did not designate Radha. Then and now, Radha has been just Radha.

I have despised 'Mrs.' for long. What do you mean by 'Mrs. Kanaran' and so on? Why can't a Cherootty or Kunhamma stay as Cherootty and Kunhamma? After marriage they turn into 'Mrs. Chappan' or [Mrs.] Korappan. Reform, indeed! It's as if women earn equality with men hanging behind them. Is this the only difficulty? If Kanaran dies today, Kanaran's wife will wed an Ambu tomorrow. Then yesterday's Mrs. Kanaran will become today's Mrs. Ambu. Not to be stopped, the day after, she accepts a Koppan. And then? She must become Mrs. Koppan. If this is so, friends, how many times should a woman change her name? Is this reform?[2] The difficulty doesn't stop there either. Suppose someone who is unaware of these turnabouts writes her a letter addressed to 'Mrs. Kanaran'? Poor old Koppan, how miserable would he feel? Can't that Cherootty keep her own name? All I feel for the admirers of such reform is disgust and dislike. And not to speak of the trouble when someone has many wives. 'Mrs.', each and everyone!

I have no doubt that freedom is necessary for women. We definitely need freedom, education and respect in the community. To that extent I go along with the advocates of reform. Yet there is a point to be made. Where does our dignity lie? Is there dignity in wandering about begging in the streets? No. What, then? If we cover ourselves from head to toe, with slits for the eyes and all wrapped up airtight like the women of the Mohammedan notables, will we be dignified? No! That can never be so. I see dignity in that older system that is neither of these: in the position of the *travattamma*.[3] It is not as if we should not interact with anyone. We may meet together and talk with others. We may manage affairs and gather news of the world. Only that we must desist from ranting and raving in destructive crowds.

Education? That is necessary. But not the education to become nurses, teachers or clerks. What we need is education that will help us to raise our children properly, guide our husbands wisely and manage the affairs of the family efficiently. It must be understood that managing the home is not simply to cook and eat. Cooking and eating is but a minor element in family management.

The position of the taravattamma has been lost in reform. Now, her place is occupied by the maid, and that of the Head of the Household is taken by the manservant. Thus our friends live, as slaves to these people. In my opinion, we ought to display our pride and freedom in matters such as these. Mrs. Cousins,[4] Sant Nihal Singh[5] and others praise the freedom of Malayali women generously. The last Women's Conference proudly publicized the incomparable freedom of the women of Kerala.[6] It should never be forgotten that it was the dignity and grandeur of the taravattammas that earned us such praise. Only such education that serves to preserve the greatness of our tradition will prove necessary and desirable for us: this I repeat.

From 'Pennungalum Parishkaravum: Avashyavum Anavasyavumaya Karyangal', 'Vanita Lokam-Anyapatrangal' (a special column that covered news and articles by women and about them in other publications). *The Mahila*, 16, 3 (March 1936): 86–88. Reprinted most probably from the *Manorama* (published from Calicut [Kozhikode]).

Notes

1 Adding the husband's or father's name to a woman's name was relatively rare in early twentieth-century Malayali society. It was among the newly-educated elite that such practice caught on. Women who used their husband's name sometimes did revert to their maiden names in writing. In this volume, we have two authors who do so: Mrs. K. Kannan Menon (Edattatta Rugmini Amma), and Mrs. C. Kuttan Nair (Kochattil Kalyanikutty Amma) also wrote under their maiden names.

2 This article really expresses an orientation that is rather different from many of the prominent reformisms of early twentieth-century Kerala, in that it seems to take easy divorce and remarriage for granted, as something readily available. Besides the change of name is taken as an embarrassment for the second husband and not for the woman herself. Early twentieth-century Malayali reformisms were highly critical of leaving the marital tie loose as the matrilineal family forms that prevailed among many groups in Kerala did.

3 Refers to the mother, usually the senior-most woman in the matrilineal joint family, which survived roughly up to the mid-twentieth century in Kerala, despite successive legislative measures from the early decades of the twentieth century onwards. There is now interesting work on the axes of authority and gender relations within the pre-colonial taravad (the matrilineal homestead), gender relations, and their transformation in the nineteenth century. See Schneider and Gough 1961; Mencher 1965; Fuller 1976; Moore 1983; Arunima 1996; 2003; Saradamoni 1999; Kodoth 1998.

4   Margaret Cousins (1878–1954) was co-founder of the Irish Women's Franchise League in 1903, and after emigrating to India in 1913, she formed the Indian Women's Association in 1917, and started the first All-India Women's Conference in 1928.
5   Probably a reference to Nihal Singh Kairon (1863–1928), pioneer of women's education in the Punjab.
6   The All-India Women's Conference held at Thiruvananthapuram in 1935. The reference was perhaps to matrilineal women, who had some more control over their lives than others like the Malayala Brahmin women or Muslim women.

27

Ayesha Mayan

Ayesha Mayan was born at Talasherry, in north Malabar, in 1914. Her father was Vayaprath Kunnath Mayan Sahib, well known during the Khilafat agitation in Malabar. She studied in Queen Mary's College, Chennai (Madras), and in St. Joseph's College, Bangalore, and was known as a brilliant student, a good public speaker, and an accomplished tennis player. She was one of the earliest Muslim women to earn a university degree in Malabar, securing the highest marks among women students from Malabar. She worked in Malabar as an instructor in the women teachers' training school, as an assistant school inspectress and as the Mappila Education Officer for Malabar and South Canara. She was active as a propagator of women's education, and headed the Kottayam Mahila Samajam in Malabar. In 1944, after her marriage, she migrated to Sri Lanka.

Our Duty

Though there are many who toil for the advancement of Womankind, few follow a constructive programme. Womankind constitutes half of humanity. Its depressed condition will have an adverse impact upon all humankind.

Womenfolk must necessarily acquire extensive knowledge. Our duty in the matter of education does not cease with arranging for the schooling of young girls. Sisters who wish to serve society, who desire the well-being of the nation must work to educate the older women. As long as the mothers who bring forth the citizens of the future remain steeped in ignorance and superstition, other reformist efforts are bound to prove unproductive. A woman bereft of good sense and education will not be of help to Man; she will turn out to be a burden.

The Koran says that women have rights just as men have. Islam dictates that women are not the instruments of male whim; it even says that they are equals, as twins are. Men have to toil ceaselessly under the pressures and burdens imposed by life because women do not do enough. How hard a man must work each day, to maintain and satisfy a wife who constantly demands fancy clothes and ornaments! This must surely change. Womenfolk must realize that just as the husband is obliged to support the wife, the wife is also bound to support the husband, partake and help in all his activities. We know that women are capable of undertaking all the activities performed by men. If, until now, we were used to employing our hands to caress Man's feet, we must now apply them to cool his brain and wipe his sweat.

In the future, we shall not be slaves, circumscribed or frail. We must prove ourselves as co-workers ready to help Man in any field, anywhere. This is the message of freedom of the twentieth century. However, there are a few women and men in our land who have imbibed such consciousness. The wheel of time will not pause for us. I have a request to make to my sisters. You must organize and work to uplift the womenfolk of your land. It is the duty of every woman to attend women's meetings and be active as much as she can. Women are often shy when it comes to attending meetings. Yet they do not find it difficult to throng crowded bazaars and shops, or wriggle into crammed vehicles. Though women are provided with separate seating space in meetings, they are reluctant about attending them. The evil customs prevalent among us today, which spring from ignorance, are causing us great vexation and ruin. Therefore we must shed our languor at least now, and strive as far as possible for our common welfare. Therefore I pray that women must awake and act.

From 'Nammude Karttavyam', *Muslim Vanita*, 1, 5, M.E. 1113, Karkatakom (Jul-Aug 1938): 133–34.

28

M. Haleema Beevi

M. Haleema Beevi (1920–2000) was born in Adoor in Travancore (Tiruvitamkoor). She and her sister were sent to school, quite against the normal practice for Muslim girls, and she studied up to the fifth class, braving stone-throwing hooligans and other such deterrents. Married at the age of sixteen, she was encouraged in her public activities by her husband, who was close to prominent Muslim reformers of the time like Vakkom Abdul Khader Moulavi. She ran a magazine for women, the Muslim Vanita *in the late 1930s, which later appeared under the name* Vanita. *In the 1940s, she started another publication, the* Bharatachandrika, *which was quite successful as a weekly, but ran into serious financial problems when it was converted into a daily. She left journalism in 1947 to make a brief attempt again in 1970, with a magazine titled* Adhunika Vanita, *which, however, proved unsuccessful. She ran a press at Tiruvalla, and during the late 1930s, the period of persecution under Dewan C. P. Ramaswamy Iyer's dictatorial regime in Travancore; she learnt printing, composing and binding to print leaflets and other material for the protesters. She was a member of the Municipal Board of Tiruvalla, the first Muslim woman to become a Municipal Councillor, the president of the Tiruvalla Muslim Women's Association, and an active member of the Muslim Majlis.*

Welcome Speech

Respected Sisters! Peace be upon you!

Today, we have here the prospect of experiencing the blessed beauty of a unique beatitude, of the priceless bonds of sisterhood. That we, who have been consigned to the depths of ignorance, who have been subsumed, immobilized, under the waves of darkness in the kitchen of unfreedom, who are not free to move out of inner quarters, or reflect on the various strands of opinion, who live lives as slaves of the worst sort, have been able to organize a conference like this, that is precisely the essence of that great beauty.

It is a terrible realization for us that if histories sought to describe groups of people who have not even been touched by civilization in this twentieth century, in which enlightenment has reached its zenith, the first place would be occupied by Muslim women. Few words will suffice to show that the demonic age of decline has left us most degraded, when we see that we are unable to step into a moral path of life for the good of one's nation, one's community and one's own siblings.

How can a community become cultured, when women, yes, women, who are the very source and essence of all the advancements of the world, have become shallow and insignificant, and bear the ill fame of being weak? The nation is not for Man alone. Woman has the right to share equally in all the duties that fall upon Man as an individual; this can never be obscured. Sacred Islam does not bar our freedom, refinement or education. Born in a time when the world had acquiesced to opinions such as 'women do not have souls; no freedom; no hope of salvation; no rights in the family', and so on, in a country in which the birth of a female infant was such ignominy to the family that it was buried alive, what did Rasool Kareem (may his name be honoured) do?

How did the Blessed One save womankind, which had been treated worse than domestic animals? Women are men's sisters. The fruit of goodness and badness in both are the same. They too have souls. How marvellous were the changes wrought in the world by such worthy teachings! Today, there are few communities that have esteemed womankind, as has Sacred Islam. Rasul Kareem's declaration that heaven lies at the feet of one's mother does us proud. When this is the reality, how pathetic is our present condition! In a community in which women languish behind the bars of unfreedom, men can never enjoy the beautiful fruits of their labours. If the world, which ought to become ever more resplendent with the radiance of the intellects of future citizens, must remain in obeisance of young people and infants fit only to be burdens upon the face of the earth, it will naturally become wan and dull.

You cannot afford to forget the fact that 'the hand that rocks the cradle, rules the world'. If we are to have erudite and cultured citizens, then those qualities must be dissolved in the very breast milk that they are fed. Surely, it is mothers who must raise them up to be citizens. When we see that the truth is that no other women are under such bondage as are women of our community, we feel ashamed about the culture of the Muslims. We should not allow ourselves to subsist on others' labours anymore, our womanliness devastated, and remain in chains, restricted, to disfigure our community and our brothers. It is but the truth that a woman can work much more effectively for the betterment of the community, than a man can. Our brothers may take very long to grasp this truth. When we come forward with unblemished ideals and competence in activity, they will honour us, strewing flowers in our path.

These sorts of thoughts now arise in us precisely because many of us, for whom the knowledge of letters was considered forbidden and criminal, have now attained education. It is a relief that today the misunderstanding that education will lead women astray has largely waned. Education has helped us to expand our ideas, express our opinions, and pronounce them. I do not forget that the large heartedness inherent in the great power of education is what has brought together all of us, who have never before stepped out, to take part in this assembly, braving fear and shame. As an enlightened group, our worthy plans of action cannot be realized by merely attending schools. We have the right to make explicit our needs and our rights. Never forget that if Man struggles to bear the burden of life, Woman is bound to bear the burden of the family. For all of Man's labours to culminate in success, Woman's sympathetic blessings are necessary. What are we to do in our lives? How may we attain [those goals]? We have several sisters who are blessed with learning and purity of ideals. It is essential that we must make the opportunity to interact closely with them, and emulate them. There is no other event that would fulfil this need better than a conference. I would like to humbly state that I have come forward to organize this conference to bolster the sense of self-respect that we, who have been suffering for long and are depressed in many ways, ought to possess.

I do feel that the profound desire to form an All-Travancore [Tiruvitamkoor] Muslim Women's Association is rather too much. But as far as we are concerned, it is imperative. I am not sure that very many will come forward to support such a venture, even if we scour the whole of Travancore. It is also quite difficult to bring them all together in practical terms. However, a common organization has become necessary for us. I would plead that women's associations must be formed in every taluk, every *kara* [a local geographical subdivision]. Our goal will be fulfilled if we have one sensible sister working in each area.

Conjoining such unions, it will not be difficult to organize an All-Travancore, or even a National Conference, without much effort. Without such an association, it will be difficult to disclose the worthiness of the Muslim women of Travancore. I do believe that the sisters gathered here today will not forget that their highest duty is to form associations in their localities, to refine the minds of their sisters.

Honourable sisters, as the formation of this association is a major event, I request you never to to show reluctance in sending our little girls, who are the crowning jewels of the family, to schools.[1] Our truthful religion and our blessed Rasool Kareem (may his name be honoured) have never regarded women as a lower race. The first Divine Message received by our Prophet bears witness to this. Do contemplate on the mystery of the injunction in the Sacred Koran 'to read in the name of your God, who has taught you to write with a pen'.

The major path in education is learning to read and write. Remember the Prophet's words about the duties of a father: 'Teach the child to write; give it a good name; conduct its marriage at the right age.' It is clear from all this that religion has not barred education. Our association is not merely for education alone. Familiarizing our girls with hygiene, how to take care of children, domestic management and literary pursuits for spiritual pleasure and self-refinement, petitioning the government about our depressed condition in education and employment and other such things figure among our goals. It is true that only the infant who cries aloud is put to the breast. However, these are times, when it seems there is no time to be fed even if one cries. We will get nothing unless we cry incessantly, and secure our needs by demanding them. The government, being engrossed in many things, cannot be expected to give us special consideration. All of us who have passed exams must put in applications for jobs. I do not intend to put forth a plan for representation, or claim. Our state shines from the rising of our blood too. It is also our duty to serve it. We too must pray for, work for, the welfare of our Maharaja. It is a great honour for us to accept employment in our country. I argue that we women must take up employment to foster our sense of self-respect. The government must also make some special arrangements for us. Our well-beloved Maharaja, who is great and noble, his minister, who is ever vigilant of the well-being of the state and other lovers of the state, will only be happy about it. For the time being, the government will have to regard our willingness and capability to be the equivalent of certificates and degrees.

Since there is not even the glimmer of a general awakening amongst Muslim women in this country, the onus of generating patriotism and loyalty is upon enlightened sisters. We are in urgent need of an association, the activities of which will be so vital that the community will be aglow in the radiance of the compassion that teems in each of us and of the bonds of our sisterhood. You have assembled here today in full recognition of this fact, shattering the strong walls of orthodoxy, walking fearlessly through the avenues of convention, wearing the crown of thorns of sacrifice. This sister of yours is powerless to express the gratitude that rises up for you from the very bottom of her heart, yet even as I admit this, I extend a hearty welcome to all of you.

(Welcome speech at Muslim Women's Conference of the Travancore (Tiruvitamkoor) Muslim Women's Association, Tiruvalla, 15 Edavam (May–June 1938). *Muslim Vanita*, 1, 4, M.E. 1113 Mithunam (June-July 1938): 103–07.[2]

Notes

1 The Conference was presided over by Mrs. Maiteen Beevi, who was the first to pass the Rashtrabhasha Visharad exam among Muslim women in Travancore. She spoke on 'Muslim Women and Modern Life', which was a strong plea for Muslim women's education and employment, as quite within Islam; indeed she argued that purdah was anti-Islamic (*Muslim Vanita*,1, 4, 1938: 107–11). Some two hundred women attended the Conference, and resolutions passed requested concessions for the education of Muslim girls, and demand for government employment. There were also resolutions requesting the government to absorb into the Travancore Government Service Dr. Habsha Maraikkar, who was the first Muslim woman from this state to earn an M.B.B.S. degree, and Mrs. Maiteen Beevi.

2 In 1891, literate women constituted a mere 1.65 percent of all the Muslim women in Travancore (*Report on the Census of Travancore* 1891, Part 2: 493). In 1931, it had gone up to just 3.1 percent (*Report on the Census of Travancore* 1931: 290).

29

Kochattil Kalyanikutty Amma

Kochattil Kalyanikutty Amma (1908-1997), also known as Mrs. C. Kuttan Nair, was born at Trichur (Thrissur). She graduated in science subjects from Queen Mary's College, Madras D, and had a long career as a teacher, which proved quite turbulent, especially towards the end. She was prominent as a contributor to magazines and known for her keen interest in women's education, active participation in the All-India Women's Conferences and support for contraception. Her travelogue, Njan Kanda Europe *(The Europe I Saw), written in the 1930s, was widely read. In 1991, she published her autobiography titled* Pathikayum Vazhiyoratte Manideepangalum (The Traveller and the Wayside Lamps), *which won the Kerala Sahitya Akademi's award for best autobiography in 1993.*

Some Obstacles in the Way of Equality between the Sexes

A certain savant has remarked that Man can look upon Woman only as 'the amalgamation of the Goddess and the Fool'. This is indeed the truth. Though women in particular countries in particular times have indeed achieved progress somewhat, womankind is still to earn equal status with men even today. Nevertheless, the numbers of women who desire such equality have been steadily on the rise. There are, however, certain impediments in the path of the equality of the sexes. Women ought to be aware of these.

First, the willingness to view life rationally is a primary requirement in today's world. From ancient times, men have associated women with the malevolent and secret arts. This association is rooted in the mind's tendency to fear the inscrutable, trapped as it is between the sensory and the extra-sensory. The mystery of the rhythms of the female body—menstruation, pregnancy, and childbirth—challenged the human powers of comprehension. Consequently, the male imagination associated Woman with sorcery and the black arts. Woman, being steeped in ignorance like Man himself, accepted this label graciously. Later, in different times and in different societies, some women did gain power and dignity as individuals, though as a group, women remained powerless. However, it is doubtful whether contemporary Man has attained significantly higher levels of psychological refinement in comparison with the tribal forest dwellers. Early memories and the doubts and horrors associated with them remain embedded in the human heart. Where the instincts and tradition hold the upper hand, objective observation and rational philosophy cannot thrive. Therefore, the amicable nature and the inclination to cooperate, that form the foundations of equality, do not materialize. This insight provides us a key to understanding why Woman is perceived to be a concoction of the Goddess and the Devil.

The fear of Woman's dark powers that sprung up so vigorously within ancient Man have condensed into certain misgivings in the Unconscious of modern Man. Contemporary socio-economic conditions have served only to aggravate such apprehensions. Today, it is common for Man to regard Woman, who is ready to work for lower wages, as his adversary. As a result, he is suspicious of all her activities. Psychologists warn that fear is harmful; though one does not know whether this hold good for all sorts of fear, it is certain that the fear of the slave experienced by the master is destructive to both. One of the major hurdles towards the equality of the sexes

SOME OBSTACLES IN THE WAY OF EQUALITY BETWEEN THE SEXES | 179

is that at present Reason is not accorded prime status. The oppression of the Jews in Germany, and the massive losses suffered by the Women's movement there are the outcomes of the displacement of Reason in that country.

Secondly, equality between the sexes is not possible without some degree of industrial culture. Muscle power ascends to prominence in a world in which mechanical devices are rejected thoroughly; this fosters the primacy of Man. If machines are proving troublesome, that is surely due to lack of appropriate regulatory efforts. Men do take pride in physical strength; let there, indeed, be abundant opportunities for the display of such strength by men. However, the industrialized countries have proved that machines controlled by the intelligence can carry out the labour performed by human muscles, and there, Woman can work alongside Man.

Thirdly, the importance that we grant today to military strength must be jettisoned completely. As long as war remains a possibility, we will continue to pay inordinate attention to militarism, military prowess and 'Manliness'. We will worship as our leader precisely that person who exemplifies these three qualities. Adverse circumstances do not permit many Joan of Arcs amongst us. Even that heroine had to encounter many obstacles, because of her sex. Today, most men consider it an insult to acknowledge a female leader. However, given the situation in which every country remains rapt on amassing the instruments of war, the day in which the immense value granted to military power will evaporate seems quit distant. By nature, women are far more reluctant to destroy life. Nevertheless, the possibility that men may develop that capacity in the future cannot be ruled out. But the National Weeks and warmongering rampant in countries like Germany, Italy and Ireland today are certainly not helpful here.

Fourthly, every woman must have access to full knowledge of contraception.[1] It makes no difference whether this is achieved through self-control, or through other means. Whatever be this, unexpected pregnancy is certainly a major hindrance for women seeking to plan and order their lives and discharge the tasks of citizenship in an uninterrupted fashion, like men. Mothers should decide for themselves the number of children they would like to have. The pro-natalist system of rewards instituted by Hitler and Mussolini rests upon the thought that 'if the Woman fills the cradle, we can conquer the world'.

Above all, our social, economic and political institutions must be thoroughly dismantled and recast. When many workers roam around helplessly without work, many others toil the whole day for a pittance. Also very many high-placed political experts overwork themselves without any sort of relaxation to the detriment of both mind and body. Without finding a solution for all this, it is difficult to attain social well-being. If everyone were assigned lighter workloads, the overburdened mothers of the present may get enough leisure and comfort in life. Those who have a penchant for homely affairs may remain snug within the home. For other, hotels, community kitchens, or nursery schools, now widely prevalent in modern countries, will be of immense help. In today's Soviet Russia, it is quite common for men to do housework. In some parts of America too, men have begun to get involved in the performance of domestic duties. In any case, unmarried women can help housewives who carry heavy loads. Even in today's Germany, young women visit the homes of busy mothers and help in bathing the children, cooking, and cleaning, under the initiative of the Women's movement. They also offer considerable help to farmers in the fields.

Of what use is equality? This may appear a legitimate question. Many of us women do firmly believe that it will alleviate much of the malaise that plagues us now. Women who advocate the equality of the sexes do not certainly want one single model to suit everyone. On the contrary, only equality will nurture uniquely individual qualities. We still possess only incomplete knowledge of our natures and dispositions. What do we actually mean by vague terms like 'Manliness' and 'Womanliness'? Does not research into psychology reveal our ignorance regarding aspects of sex difference? How many individuals are left stunted by our moral precepts, which are the offspring of our half-baked knowledge!

In human society with rational orientation, we would behave more considerately towards each other. There, neither class nor caste nor position would matter; the greatness of the mind will form the sole criterion of valuation. When individual greatness is recognized as superior to community and tradition, the importance we now concede to external physical differences will wither away. In such a world, many-splendoured individuality, unthinkable in today's world of hatred and negative attitudes, may materialize, and along with it, happiness and contentment. In such a society the question 'what for the equality of the sexes?' may echo as meaningless noise.

From 'Streepurushasamatvattinulla Chila Pratibandhangal', *Matrubhumi* (weekly), special issue 1938, article no. 12.

Note

1 It may be mentioned here that contraception, especially contraceptive devices, was a hotly-debated topic in Travancore, Cochin and Malabar in the 1930s, for instance, in the All-India Women's Conference held at Thiruvananthapuram in 1935. Kochattil Kalyanikutty Amma was well known as an ardent champion of birth control, and indeed, was mercilessly lampooned by sections of the press for this. See 'Matrubhumiyile Gandhijiyum Mrs. Nairute Avashatayum' (Gandhiji in the *Matrubhumi* and Mrs. Nair's Infirmity), *Navasarasan*, 2, 3 and 4 (1936–37): 5–6.

References

Anandi, T. K. 2002. 'Local History of Women's Participation in the Freedom Movement and Socio-Political Movement in Malabar: Analysis and Documentation'. Project Report submitted to Kerala Research Programme on Local-Level Development. Centre for Development Studies, Thiruvananthapuram.

Antharjanam, K. Lalithambika. 1952: *Moodupadattil*. Kottayam: SPSS, 1952.

Arunima, G. 1996. 'Multiple Meanings: Changing Conceptions of Matriliny Kinship in Nineteenth- and Twentieth-Century Malabar', *Indian Economic and Social History Review* 33, 3: 283–307.

———. 2003. *There Comes Papa: Colonialism and the Transformation of Matriliny in Kerala, Malabar c. 1850–1940*. New Delhi: Orient Longman.

Ayyappan, Sahodaran K. 1965. *Saddesheeyam*, Ernakulam.

Babu, I. V. 2001: *Keraleeya Navotdhanavum Nambutirimarum*, Kottayam: Sahitya Pravartaka Sahakarana Sangham.

Chaitanya, Krishna. 1971. *A History of Malayalam Literature*. New Delhi: Orient Longman.

Devika, J. 1999. *En-Gendering Individuals: The Language of Re-forming in Early Twentieth Century Kerala*. New Delhi: Orient Longman, 2007.

———. 2003. 'Beyond *Kulina* and *Kulata*: The Critique of Gender Difference in the Writings of K. Saraswati Amma', *Indian Journal of Gender Studies* 10, 2: 210–28.

Fuller, C. J. 1976. *The Nayars Today*. Cambridge: Cambridge University Press.

Innes, C. A., and F. B. Evans, eds. 1951 rpt. (1908) *Madras District Gazetteers: Malabar*, Madras: Madras Government Press.

Irumbayam, P. V. George. 1985. *Nalu Novelukal* (Four Novels). Thrissur: Kerala Sahitya Akademi.

Jeffrey, Robin. 2003. *Politics, Women and Well-Being*. Basingstoke, Hampshire: Macmillan.

Kodoth, Praveena. 1998. 'Women and Property Rights: A Study of Land Tenure Structure and Personal Law in Malabar 1890–1940'. Ph.D. Diss. Department of Economics, University of Hyderabad.

———. 2001.' Courting Legitimacy or Delegitimizing Custom? Sexuality, *Sambandham*, and Marriage Reform in Late Nineteenth-Century Malabar. *Modern Asian Studies* 35, 2: 349–84.

———. 2002. 'Gender, Community and Identity in Christian Property Law Reform: The Case of Early Twentieth-Century Tiruvitamkoor', *Inter-Asia Cultural Studies* 3, 3: 383–93.

Kumar, Udaya. 1997. 'Self, Body and Inner Sense: Some Reflections on Sree Narayana Guru and Kumaran Asan', *Studies in History* n.s. 13, 2: 247–70.

Lindberg, Anna. 2001. 'Experience and Identity: A Historical Account of Class, Caste and Gender among the Cashew Workers of Kerala 1930–2000.' PhD Diss, Lund University.

Marath, S. Menon. 1960. *The Wound of Spring.* London: Dennis Dobson.

Mencher, Joan. 1965. 'The Nayars of South Malabar'. In *Comparative Family Systems*, edited by M. F. Nimkoff. Boston: Houghton Mifflin.

Menon, P. K. K. 1972. *The History of the Freedom Movement in Kerala*, vol.2. Thiruvananthapuram: Government of Kerala.

Moore, Melinda. 1983. 'Taravad: House, Land and Relationships in a Hindu Matrilineal Society', Ph.D. Diss. Department of Anthropology, University of Chicago.

Nair, N. Balakrishnan. 1947. *K. Chinnamma: Oru Jeevacharitram* (K. Chinnamma: A Biography). Thiruvananthapuram: Srivilas Press.

Nair, K. Maheshwaran, ed. 1995. *Chattambi Swamikal: Jeevitavum Kritikalum.* Thiruvananthapuram: Bhooma Books.

Nair, P. K. Parameshwaran. 1972. *Sahityapanchananan.* Kottayam: Sahitya Pravarttaka Sahakarana Sangham.

Nair, S. Guptan, ed. 1979. *Kuttikunhu Tangachiyude Kritikal.* Thrissur: Kerala Sahitya Akademi.

Perumtottam, Joseph, ed. 1999. *Mar Charles Lavigne – Jeevacharitravum Idayalekhanangalum*, Changanashery: HIRS Publications.

Pillai, T. K. Velu, ed. 1996 rpt. (1940). *Travancore State Manual*, vols. 1 and 2. Thiruvananthapuram: Kerala State Gazetteers.

Pisharoty, Cherukad Govinda. 1984. *Jeevitapata*, Thiruvananthapuram: Deshabhimani.

Priyadarshan, G. 1982: *Malayala Patrapravarttanam: Prarambha Swaroopam*, Thrissur: Kerala Sahitya Akademi.

Raghavan, Putupally. 1985. *Kerala Patrapravarttana Charitram.* Thrissur: Kerala Sahitya Akademi.

Rajeevan, B. 1999. 'From Caste to Sex: A Study on Sexuality and the Formation of the Modern Subject in Kerala'. In *Rethinking Development: Kerala's Development Experience*, M. A. Oomen, ed., New Delhi: Concept: 45–59.

Raveendran, N. K. 1992. 'Streevimochanattinte Prasnangal Malayala Sahityattil' (Problems of Women's Literature in Malayalam Literature), Ph.D. Diss., University of Kerala, Thiruvananthapuram.

Ravindran, T. K. 1975. *Vaikom Satyagraha and Gandhi.* Thrissur: Sree Narayana Institute of Social and Cultural Development.

Report of the Malabar Marumakkathayam Commission, Madras: Government of Madras, 1891 Sanjayan (M.R.Nair). 1970. *Sanjayan-1936le Hasyalekhanangal*, Kozhikode: Matrubhumi.

Saradamoni, K. 1999. *Matriliny Transformed: Family, Law and Ideology in Twentieth-Century Travancore*. New Delhi: Sage.

Schneider, D. M., and Kathleen Gough, eds. 1961: *Matrilineal Kinship*, Berkeley: University of California Press.

Scott, Joan W. 2001. 'Fantasy Echo: History and the Construction of Identity', *Critical Inquiry* 27: 284–306.

Singh, K. S., ed. 2002. *People of India – Kerala*, vol. 27, Part 2. Chennai: Affiliated East-West Press.

Subramoniam, V. I., ed. 1993. *Dravidian Encyclopaedia*, vol. 2. Thiruvananthapuram: International School of Dravidian Linguistics.

Ulakamtara, Mathew. 1995. *I.C.Chacko*. Thiruvananthapuram: Department of Cultural Publications, Government of Kerala.

Unemployment Enquiry Committee Report of Travancore. 1928. Thiruvananthapuram: Government Press.

Velayudhan, Meera. 1999. 'Reform, Law and Gendered Identity'. In *Rethinking Development : Kerala's Development Experience*, M. A. Oommen, ed., Delhi: Concept: 60–72.

———. 1999. 'Growth of Political Consciousness among Women in Modern Kerala'. In *Perspectives in Kerala History*, P. J. Cheriyan, ed., Thiruvananthapuram: Kerala State Gazetteers.

Who's Who of Freedom Fighters in Kerala. 1975. Thiruvananthapuram: Government of Kerala.

Additional Readings

When *Her-Self* appeared in 2005, the field of gender history in Kerala was still quite unexplored. However, many exciting things were happening in the 1990s and after, and these came to flower in the first decade of the new millennium. Important work was published, which tackled older, more familiar, questions, such as that of matriliny and women's agency in Kerala, as well as ones which advanced new proposals for histories of gender. Feminist historians were beginning to question deeply the dominant narratives about social reformism in twentieth-century Kerala in the 1990s, for example, Toshie Awaya's essay on Malayala Brahmin reformism: 'Women in the Nambutiri "Caste" Movement'. In T. Mizushima and H. Yanagisawa, eds., *History and Society in South India* (Tokyo: Tokyo University of Foreign Studies, 1994): 47–57. Awaya's themes have been fruitfully extended through an interdisciplinary lens by Ester Gallo in her insightful *The Fall of Gods: Memory, Kinship, and Middle-Classes in South India* (Oxford: Oxford University Press, 2017).

Also, early historical work on women in twentieth-century working class mobilizations, for example, Meera Velayudhan's essay 'Caste, Class and Political Organisation of Women in Travancore' (*Social Scientist*, 19, 5/6 (1991) began to be expanded. My research which extended the inquiry about the intertwining of gender, social reform, development, and politics into the mid-twentieth century, the high noon of nationalist developmentalism, was published as *Individuals, Householders, Citizens: Malayalis and Family Planning 1930–1970* (New Delhi: Zubaan, 2008).

In the fifteen years since the publication of *Her-Self*, the most prolific area of publication relevant to themes it raised has been literary translation. The literary works of early feminists, N. Lalithambika Antharjanam and K. Saraswathi Amma are now available in translation. A fresh translation of Lalitambika's novel *Agnisakshi* by Vasanthy Sankaranarayanan is available (New Delhi: Oxford University Press, 2015); the translation of her stories and memoirs was published as *Cast Me Out If You Will: Stories and Memoir*, translated by Gita Krishnankutty (Kolkata: Stree, 1998). A newer collection of her short stories, *On the Far Side of Memory*, was translated by J. Devika (New Delhi: Oxford University Press, 2017). Translations of a selection of short stories by K. Saraswathi Amma are available on https://swatantryavaadini.in/. This website pays homage to the first-generation of modern-educated women who pushed at the boundaries with varying degrees of success. Besides, the memoirs of Devaki Nilayangode who was witness to many of the tumultuous scenes of social change in the 1940s and after has also appeared in translation: *Antharjanam: Memoirs of Namboodiri Woman* (Oxford University Press, 2011). A brief and exploratory history of gender in the Malayali literary public of the twentieth century has also appeared: *Womanwriting = Manreading?* (New Delhi: Penguin India, Zubaan, 2013).

About the Editor-Translator

J. Devika is a historian, feminist and social critic. She is Professor, Centre for Development Studies, Thiruvananthapuram. She has authored several books and articles on gender relations in early Kerala society. She has translated both fiction and non-fiction books from Malayalam and English. Among these are Nalini Jameela (*Autobiography of a Sex Worker*, Penguin) and the short stories of K. R. Meera and Sarah Joseph. She also translated the acclaimed Malayalam novel *Arrachar* by K. R. Meera as *Hangwoman* (Penguin, 2014). She writes on gender, politics, social reforms and development in Kerala on publications like *Kafila, Economic and Political Weekly* and *The Wire*. She received her MA in modern History from the Centre for Historical Studies, JNU, and obtained her PhD in History from Mahatma Gandhi University, Kottayam. She also has a website about the first generation Malayali feminists: swatantryavaadini.in